Peter, Starigrad Paklenica, 11th c.

St *John,* Preko (island of Ugljan), 11th c.

t *Francis,* dedicated 1280

Salvation Church at the source of the Cetina, 9th c.

St *Nicholas,* Split, 11th c.

St *Nicholas,* Prahulje near Nin, 12th c.

Pope John Paul II among the Croats, September 1994

HYMN TO FREEDOM

Oh beautiful, dear, sweet Freedom.
The gift in which the god above hath given us
all blessings,
Oh true cause of all our glory.
Only adorment of this Grove.
All silver, all gold, all men's lives
Could not purchase thy pure beauty!

Ivan Gundulić

Translated by Dr. E. D. Gray

Vlaho Bukovac: The Croatian National Revival, curtain in the Croatian National Theatre in Zagreb
The artist painted the poet Ivan Gundulić, the author of the Hymn To Freedom, on a throne. Before him meritorious Croats stand, as follows: Ljudevit Gaj, Antun Mihanović, Janko Drašković, Dimitrije Demeter, Ivan Mažuranić, Stanko Vraz, Mirko Bogović, Sidonija Erdödy-Rubido, Ivan Kukuljević-Sakcinski, Pavao Stoos, Petar Preradović, Antun Nemčić, Vatroslav Lisinski, Ferdo Wiesner-Livadić, Ljudevit Vukotinović, Dragutin Rakovac, Adam Mandrović, Marija Ružička-Strozzi, Josip Freudenreich

OUR LOVELY HOMELAND

Lovely are you, our dear homeland,
You beloved land of heroes.
Of the fame of our forefathers.
May you be forever honoured.

We love you for your glory
We love you as our own.
We love you for your plains,
We love you for your mountains.

Flow on Sava, flow on Drava,
And you Danube flow on strongly.
You blue sea tell all the world
How the Croats love their people.

While the sun strikes on the meadows,
While the oak bends to gales,
When the dead in graves are hidden,
While the heart alive is beating.

Antun Mihanović

Croatian national anthem
Translated by Sonia Wild-Bičanić

Zelenjak - Mihanović's valley, the monument in the honour of the poet and the Croatian national anthem he wrote

The Mihanović manor

HRVATSKA

Zagreb, 1994.

Publishers:

ITP "MARIN DRŽIĆ" d.d. Zagreb
GRAFOUSLUGA d.o.o. Zagreb

Responible for the publishers:

BORIS ZDUNIĆ

Idea, concept and get up:

DRAGO ZDUNIĆ

Editors:

MARIJAN HORVAT
DRAGO ZDUNIĆ

Technical editor:

FRANJO HLUPIĆ

Translation by:

NIKOLINA JOVANOVIĆ

Photographs by:

Arheološki muzej Zagreb, Babić Milan, Bačić Živko, Bearza Giovani, Božičević Srećko, Bralić Ivo, Buljević Zvonimir, † Čaće Nedjeljko, Čolić Marko, Čuljat Marko, Dabac Petar, † Dabac Tošo, Gelenčir Josip, Giuricin Virgilio, Grčević Mladen, Griesbach Đuro, Hreljanović Egon, Hreljanović Viktor, Huber Đuro, Kalenić Dražen, Kosinožić Renco, Krčadinac Željko, Kršćanska sadašnjost, Muzejski prostor Zagreba – Arhiva, Mjeda Luka, † Novaković Mato, † Pavić Milan, Pervan Ivo, Rastić Tomislav, † Radić Jure, Radauš-Ribarić Jelka, Strikoman Šime, Strnad Krešimir, Sušić Goran, Šporer Tomislav, Topić Marin, Virtuoso Daniel, Volarić Saša, Zahtila Elvis, Zdunić Drago, Zdunić Koraljka, Zubović Antun

ISBN 953-6069-00-8

Graphical desing:

LITOGRAF s.p.o. Zagreb

Printing and Binding:

GRAFIČKI ZAVOD HRVATSKE, Zagreb

The edition was published in 1994 ,in 20.000 copies in Croatian, English, German, and French.

CONTENTS

A page from Hrvoje's Missal

5

STATES THAT HAVE RECOGNIZED THE REPUBLIC OF CROATIA

1. ALGERIA
2. ALBANIA, Republic
3. ARGENTINA, Republic
4. AUSTRALIA
5. AUSTRIA, Republic
6. BAHRAIN
7. BELGIUM, Federation
8. BOSNIA-HERCEGOVINA, Republic
9. BELARUS, Republic
10. BOLIVIA, Republic
11. BRAZIL, Federal Republic
12. BRUNEI
13. BULGARIA, Republic
14. BURKINA FASO
15. CYPRUS, Republic
16. DENMARK, kingdom
17. CZECH REPUBLIC
18. SLOVAKIA, Republic
19. EGYPT, Arab Republic
20. ESTONIA, Republic
21. ETHIOPIA, NDR
22. PHILIPPINES, Republic
23. FINLAND, Republic
24. FRANCE, Republic
25. GHANA, Republic
26. GREECE, Republic
27. GEORGIA, Republic
28. GUATEMALA, Republic
29. CHILE, Republic
30. INDIA, Republic
31. INDONESIA, Republic
32. IRAN, Islamic Republic
33. IRELAND, Republic
34. ICELAND
35. ITALY, Republic
36. ISRAEL
37. JAMAICA
38. JAPAN
39. YEMEN
40. JORDAN, kingdom
41. REPUBLIC OF SOUTH AFRICA
42. CANADA
43. QUATAR
44. KAZAKHSTAN
45. KENYA
46. CHINA, PR
47. COLUMBIA, Republic
48. NORTH KOREA
49. SOUTH KOREA
50. CUBA, Republic
51. LITHUANIA, Republic
52. LEBANON, Republic
53. LIBYA
54. LIECHTENSTEIN, principality
55. LATVIA, Republic
56. LUXEMBURG, grand duchy
57. HUNGARY, Republic
58. MACEDONIA, Republic
59. MALAYSIA
60. MALI, Republic
61. MALTA, Republic
62. MOROCCO, kingdom
63. MAURITANIA, Islamic Republic
64. MEXICO (United States of Mexico)
65. MOLDAVIA, Republic
66. MONGOLIA, Republic
67. NIGERIA, Federal Republic
68. NETHERLANDS, kingdom
69. GERMANY, Federal Republic
70. NORWAY, kingdom
71. NEW ZEALAND
72. OMAN, sultanate
73. PAKISTAN, Islamic Republic
74. PANAMA, Republic
75. SPAIN, kingdom
76. PARAGUAY, Republic
77. PERU, Republic
78. POLAND, Republic
79. PORTUGAL, Republic
80. ROMANIA, Republic
81. RUSSIAN FEDERATION
82. UNITED STATES OF AMERICA
83. SALVADOR, Republic
84. SAN MARINO, Republic
85. SINGAPORE, Republic
86. SLOVENIA, Republic
87. SRI LANKA, Dem. Soc. Rep.
88. SUDAN, Republic
89. STATE OF VATICAN CITY
90. TAJIKISTAN, Republic
91. TANZANIA, United Republic
93. TUNISIA, Republic
94. TURKEY, Republic
95. UNITED ARAB EMIRATES
96. UKRAINE
97. URUGUAY, Oriental Republic
98. SWEDEN, kingdom
99. GREAT BRITAIN and NORTHERN IRELAND, United Kingdom
100. VENEZUELA, Republic
101. SWITZERLAND, confederation
102. ZAMBIA, Republic
103. CAPE VERDE ISLANDS
104. SAUDI ARABIA

OUR LOVELY CROATIA

A message to the reader

When you take this book into your hands and begin to go throught it, I am sure that you cannot help feeling, just as I have done, a strong sense of patriotism, of warmth and of pride of our lovely homeland.

All nations love their homeland, whatever that homeland is like. But there can be few nations that have been able to crate a state and a cultural life in a part of the world so blessed by natural beauty and climate, so open to movement and variety, as Croatia. Through their history the Croats have been aware of the unique place they occupy. Spiritually and creatively they have known how to use the great cultures that existed within their immediate vicinity and permeated their own, yet nevertheless make their own original contribution to European culture and scholarship. The achievements shown in this book are a witness of this.

Croatia is a unique example of a small nation which for centuries bled in defence of European culture and of Christianity but which, in spite of all her historical misfortune, managed to preserve her cultural identity. Our role in, and contribution to, European culture is recorded in the stone and the written monuments of our medieval history which can stand side by side with those of even the oldest European nations.

Small European nations – like the Croats – are predestined to the hard fate of having to defend national existence, cultural identity and their identity as a state. The Croatian nation has stubbornly survived in an area exposed to the conquests of Byzantium and the Franks, the Venetians and the Turks, to German, Italian, Hungarian and most recently Serbian imperialism. It was out of the reality of this historical and geopolitical matrix that the Croat nation developed a political philosophy not of conquest and supression, but of survival through adherence to the wider ideals of coexistence, peace, openness, hospitality, Christian universalism, ecumenism, socialist internationalism, regional and European integration. These principles have sometimes been more of a disadvantage than an advantage.

It is affiliation to western civilization no less than the development of a national culture, pride and love of freedom that have enabled the Croats to survive in past and more recent historical periods. It is these things that have made it possible for them to maintain their own national existence and their own tradition as an independent state. In spite of adverse geopolitical realities which threatened complete erasement more than they did any rich interfusion of three different civilizations.

Now, for the first time in recent history, there is an unrepeatable chance for the Croatian state and Croatian culture to achieve a place of equality in the new democratic organization of Europe. True to our own history we are among the first champions of the peaceful integration of the sovereign nations of Europe. True to our own history we are among the first champions of the peaceful integration of the sovreign nations of Europe. In a Europe that is spacially and civilizationally integrated while leaving room for national individuality, Croatia will for the first time have full opportunity to realize her Central European and Mediterranean position. What is more, Croatia, in a European community created as a result of the freely chosen unfication of small and large nations, can come to play an increasingly important part internationally.

Croatia has achieved a place for herself in the new, democratic world by the convincing and peaceful way in which she is conducting the transformation of one-party, communist, totalitarianism into parliamentary democracy. Post-communist society – which means also Croatian society – is a dramatic transition moment of European history.

The creation of a free and sovereign Croatian state, following the triumphant victory of democracy in the first free elections, is a challenge for us all. I am convinced that the regenerative strength of national self-confidence together with the unquenchable creative spirit of the Croatian nation and a feeling of patriotic responsibility are guarantees for progress, peace and prosperity in this »Our lovely Croatia«.

Dr Franjo Tudman
President of the Republic of Croatia

ZVONIMIR'S BOAT

It is still here,
On this rock-strewn shore
This past eight hundred years.
Beaten from all sides,

Thrashed by
The gales, the waves the storms,
Smothered and crushed
Into the sand – Yet still here.

Vladimir Nazor
1912

OUR LOVELY CROATIA

For millennia Croats have lived in a land of unique beauty, in an area situated where the Alpine, Pannonian and Mediterranean regions of the vast Central-European geographical sphere converge resulting in a magnificent blend of plain, hill, mountain and rocky karst. This ancient Croatian land includes the endless flat fields and plough-land of Srijem and Slavonia, the central-Slavonian timbered hills edged by the Drava and Sava valleys, glades and hills of picturesque Zagorje, the forested mountains of Gorski Kotar, the hills and lowlands of Istria, the mountains and plateaus of Lika, the karstland of the Dalmatian Hinterland, the coastal belt stretching beside the blue sea, and the wonderful Adriatic islands.

Man has lived in this beautiful Croatian homeland since ancient prehistory, inhabiting the diverse expanses that include impressive mountains and vast plains, rivers and streams flowing through mountain gorges and fertile plains, areas covered by lavish vegetation and zones of naked karst, a region with one of the most beautiful coastlines. He has made use of the gifts of nature and its shelters to build homes and settlements and develop a prosperous communal life.

Prehistoric times. In the oldest period of human existence (the palaeolithic) man *(Homo primigenius)* wandered through this region hunting in the undergrowth of mountain forests and sheltering in caves and half-caves, in which the hearth meant life and safety. These primeval times left traces in Croatia. There are important finds from the Villafranchien period (2,500,000 – 800,000 BC) in the Šandalja I locality in Istria, from the mid-palaeolithic (500,000 – 100,000 BC) in the Ponikve and Golubovec localities in Croatian Zagorje and in Donje Pazarište in Lika, from the mid and late palaeolithic (150,000 – 6,000 BC) in the Hušnjakovo, Vindija, Vuglovec and Velika Pećina localities in Croatian Zagorje, in Veternica on Mount Medvednica, Zarilac in Slavonia, Vrlovka and Lovke in Gorski kotar, Cerovec cave in Lika, and Brina in the Dalmatian Hinterland. A great number of artefacts (axes, scrapers) found in these localities show the beginnings of human work and man's sense for shaping well-made and often symmetrical implements.

Discovering the use of domesticated animals, man began to breed livestock, and then to till the land and grow his own food (neolithic, 6,000 – 2,000 BC). This tied him to low-lying fertile areas where there were no suitable shelters, so he began building the first houses and hill-fort settlements for group protection.

In the neolithic continental Palaeopannonians built organized fortified settlements in the localities of Vučedol, Drenovac, Kremenjača, Šamatovci, Pepelane and Vlastelinski brijeg in Srijem and Slavonia. Only exceptionally did they continue living in caves, like in Vindija in Zagorje. Inhabitants of the coastal area, Palaeomediterraneans, built settlements in localities on the Ižula peninsula in Istria, and in the surroundings of Nin, Bribir, Sinj, Danilo Bitinja and Škrip in Dalmatia, but they also continued to live in caves like Gudnja, Pokrivenik, Kopačina and Grapčeva spilja.

At the time when man's harsh struggle for survival taught him the value of using metal (copper, bronze, iron) to produce what he needed (metal age, 2,000 BC), great ethnic changes took place in what is today Croatia as the Illyrians emerged on the scene of history. They lived in tribes, bred livestock, cultivated the soil, hunted and fished, and built numerous forts *(kasteljeri),* in the lowlands protected with earthen banks, palisades and ditches, in hilly regions by drystone ramparts. Many of these settlements assumed an urban character, like the fortified centers of Vučedol, Dalj, Sarvaš, Gardun (Srijem and Slavonia), Sveti Petar Ludbreški (Croatian Zagorje), Turska kosa (Pokuplje), Vital, Klačenica, Kuk (Lika and Primorje), Nesactium, Picugi, Vintijana (Istria), Vijenac, Ljubač, Bribir, Babina glavica, Koštilo (Dalmatia).

Production soared during that time (pottery, extracting and processing metal), goods were exchanged, and the first European trade route in this area appeared (the Amber Route), which ran along the Croatian coast connecting the Aegean with the Baltic region.

In that period utilitarian products were joined by fine artwork, stylized figures (the *Dove of Vučedol*) and stylized stone sculptures (the figure of a man and a mounted figure from Nesactium – today in the Archaeological Museum in Pula).

By the middle of the first millennium BC the Croatian coastal region had come into contact with the classical world, first with the Hellenistic, and then, at the end of the third century BC, with the Roman world. The Illyrian-Hellenistic encounter was first echoed in architecture (Cyclopean walls) in Škrip, Tor, Nesactium, Varvaria, Asseria, Nedinum and Rider, and in the finds of the oldest Hellenistic ceramics (in Nin).

The Classical Period. Immediate classical influence begin with Greek colonization (5th – 3rd century BC) and the foundation of the maritime Hellenistic emporia of Issa (Vis), Pharos (Stari Grad on the island of Hvar), Salona (Solin), Tragurion (Trogir), Epetion (Stobreč) and Epidaurus (Cavtat). Greek presence brought Hellenistic cultural influence to the eastern Adriatic coast. The first strongly fortified urban centers were built (sites of Issa and Pharos) with the regular town-plan of a rectangular castrum. An important early Greek inscription in stone – Psefism – was found in Lumbarda on the island of Korčula (Korkyra Melaina), recording the decision made during the administration of the Hieromnemon Praxidam to found the town, and listing the rights of the inhabitants who had built the town-walls.

Besides preserved architectural fragments, the high Hellenistic cultural level of this region can also be seen in surviving works of art like the exquisite bronze sculpture of the head of a goddess found in the ruins of Issa, the marble relief of Kairos from Tragurion, the rich finds of Greek sepulchral ceramics, as well as in numerous ancient-Greek texts carved in stone (the oldest description of a maritime battle between the Greeks and the Illyrians in front of Pharos).

The violent Roman conquest, which started at the end of the 3rd century BC, first overran Dalmatia and Istria and then the territory of Pannonia. The Illyrians resisted the enemy bitterly, and Queen Teuta in central Dalmatia (end of 3rd century BC), Epulus in Istria (beginning of 2nd century BC) and Bato in Pannonia (beginning of 1st century AD) waged fierce battles against them.

The Romans started building fortified strongholds in the newly-conquered lands and roads to connect them with the Apennine peninsula. Salona (Solin), Narona (Vid near Metković), Iadera (Zadar), Aenona (Nin), Pola (Pula), Parentium (Poreč), Senia (Senj), Siscia (Sisak), Mursa (Osijek), Cibalae (Vinkovci), Marsonia (Brod) and Andautonia (Šćitarjevo) were the most important fortified towns and military strongholds. Their remaining urban arrangement shows that most of them were castrums (Parentium, Iadera), and fewer developed organically (Pola).

Many monumental structures remain from this period, preserved fragmentarily or to a great degree: Diocletian's Palace in Split, the amphitheatre in Solin, fortified palaces in Polače on the island of Mljet, the forum in Zadar, the arena, theatre, temple and the Sergi triumphal arch in Pula, the temple in Poreč and *villae rusticae* on Brijuni.

Many sculptures (statues of Roman gods and emperors, tombstone reliefs, sarcophagi), wall paintings, figural and ornamental floor mosaics, as well as many metal objects, ceramics and stone inscriptions, remain from the culture of classical Rome (they are kept in archaeological museums in Zagreb, Pula, Zadar and Split or *in situ*).

In the Augustun period Roman masters modelled their style on Hellenistic harmony, whereas late-Roman art is monumental both in proportions and in ornamentation.

Late Classical Period, Early-Christian Period and the Great Migrations. Great changes in the life of this region started with the decline of the classical period: the fall of the Western Roman Empire (AD 476), the incursion of Christianity and its affirmation (the Edict of Milan – 313), and the stormy perturbations caused by medieval migrations (end 4th – 7th century). The deprived espoused Christianity, parts of the Roman provinces were overrun by new ethnic groups that found it difficult to accept the remaining classical norms so they deformed them, inevitably introducing rustic characteristics into the region that changed the customary classical postulates.

In the late classical period the rules of classical harmony deteriorated and not much was built. Almost all new building was sacral, and there are several such exceptional buildings in Croatia.

Parts of the monumental Basilica of Euphrasius in Poreč with an atrium, baptistery and consignatory, and a richly adorned interior (columns with capitals, incrustration, mosaics, stucco), date from the Early-Christian period (4th–6th century). This was a period of fascinating interiors (sacral isolation), while the exteriors of buildings were not considered important. Parts of other important Early-Christian churches have been preserved in damaged, ruined or reconstructed form, like the twin basilica of Pula Cathedral, the Basilica of Our Lady on Brijuni, St Mary's Cathedral in Krk, St John's Cathedral in Rab, the substructure of St Anastasia's Cathedral in Zadar, the complex of basilicas (Constantine's, Urban's and of the Holy Cross) with a baptistery in Solin, basilicas on the localities of Manastirine, Marusinac and Kapljuč in the Solin area, St Ciprian's basilica in Gate, St Peter's in Stonsko polje, the basilica in Polače on the island of Mljet, the substructure of St Mary's Cathedral in Dubrovnik, St John the Baptist's on Brač and many others built in towns and the country.

During this period (4th/5th–7th/8th centuries) new tribes from continental east Europe (Huns, Visigoths, Ostrogoths, Lombards, Gepids, Avars, Slavs-Croats) migrated into these Roman provinces bringing with them their own creative traditions, and gradually adopting elements of a strong classical influence enhanced by Christianity.

Early-Croatian Period. Early medieval migrations included those of Slav clans, who after their diaspora in the middle of the first millennium arrived in the Roman Pannonian-Dalmatian region at the end of the 6th and the beginning of the 7th century. From the 7th to the 12th century they formed the Croatian national community in that region and organized the Croatian state.

In this period the Croats lived a very active social, political, cultural and art life, documented in the first period (7th–8th century) by sepulchral finds in Čađavica (Slavonia), Čelega (Istria), Biskupija and Dubravice (Dalmatia). After that (8th–9th century) they built a large number of fortified towns (Mrsunjski lug, Sveti Petar Ludbreški, Spačva), royal residences (*curtis*) in Nin, Knin, Biograd na moru, Bijači and Klis and, finally, a sequence of exquisite Early-Croatian churches. These were built in the spirit of their own tradition in contact with Byzantine influence, the classical Roman heritage and Frankish influence. They had diverse ground plans and structural elements, varying from simple single-nave basilicas and unpretentious centrally-planned structures to developed basilicas with two or three aisles, and monumental rotondas.

The most important architecture of the Early-Croatian period includes churches: St Barbara in Trogir, St Petar Stari, St Laurence and St Donatus in Zadar, the Holy Trinity, St Martin and Sv Mikula in Split, St Peter in Priko near Omiš, St George in Rovanjska, St Donatus, St Chrysogonous and St Lucy of Jurandvor on the island of Krk, St Nicolas, St Luke and the Sigurata on Prijeko in Dubrovnik and many others built along the Croatian Adriatic shore.

These churches exhibit the innate Early-Croatian creative vision which in fact overpowered and absorbed the existing Roman, Byzantine and Frankish influences subordinating them to the elementary rustic concepts of native craftsmen. Many of these churches were adorned with plaited ornamentation and with inscriptions engraved in the stone inventory, giving the names of Croatian district prefects, abbots, princes and kings. Besides many inscriptions in Latin (inscriptions mentioning Prince Branimir: in Muč from 888, in Nin where he was called the Prince of the Slavs, in Šopot where he was called the Prince of the Croats – the first appearance of the Croatian name carved in a stone document; the inscription of Queen Jelena from 976), in the Early-Croatian period there were also inscriptions in the Croatian language and in the Glagolitic alphabet (the Baška Tablet from the end of the 11th century mentioning »... the Croatian King Zvonimir ...«). This shows that the creative opus of the Early-Croatian period belongs to the highest reaches of medieval European culture and art.

When the life of Croats in their new homeland grew more stable they built villages and towns. In the beginning the clans built on naturaly protected clearings, in forests or on raised ground surrounded by marshes, near fertile land and forests that provided them with the essentials for their life of cattle-breeders and farmers. These settlements became the centers of the clan's economic and cultural life and roads linked them with their broader environs.

The urban heritage from earlier classical and early-medieval periods differed in the Dalmatian-Istrian and the Slavonian region. Coastal areas had suffered less destruction during the great migrations and towns were built of stone so urban life in the coastal classical town communes (Poreč, Pula, Krk, Senj, Zadar, Trogir, Split, Stari Grad, Cavtat) continued during the arrival and settlement of Slavs-Croats in their new homeland and during the formation of the Croatian state. The classical towns of the continental region (Sisak, Vinkovci, Osijek, Brod, Ludbreg), however, were gradually destroyed during the conquest and due to less durable building material.

These were the circumstances under which the Croats built their first settlements along the Adriatic coast, initially isolated and in the middle of small fertile regions. These first settlements included Stari Gorčan, Rogatica, Dragozetić and Orlec in Istria and the Kvarner region, Biograd, Rižinice, Dubravice, Tinj, Šibenik, and towns built on the remains of old settlements like Bribir, Knin and Nin, in Dalmatia. After initial stabilization the Croats gradually began to settle the old urban communes, too, and these remained the centres of life in this area. In the continental (Slavonian) region, on the contrary, the administrative and economic function of the first Croatian district centres and market-towns grew stronger and they became important factors in feudal development. In time (13th–14th century) royal charters were conferred on them giving them the privileges of free royal market-places or towns. These were Varaždin, Perna, Vukovar, Virovitica, Petrinja, Samobor, Zagreb's Gradec, Križevci, Jastrebarsko, Zelina, Trg under Ozalj, Krapina and Koprivnica.

It must finally be said that in the Early-Croatian period the strength of Croatian national and cultural identity – especially present in the wider European circle (*Papal letters,* 9th c., *De administrando imperio* by Constantine Porphyrogentius, mid-10th c.) after their conversion (9th century) – was permanently expressed in the cohesion of the ethnic community and in the vitality with which they absorbed and adapted influences. Thus the Croats retained their origial name in the overall medieval ethnic transformation of tribal structures, and it has remained their national name until the present day.

Medieval Period. Great changes took place on the territory of what is today Croatia after Early-Croatian state independence was transformed through the union of the Croatian and Hungarian crowns in 1102.

In that crucial period the elementary indigenous Early-Croatian cultural forcelines encountered, and were partly assimilated by, strong West-European and Central-European cultural influences. This cultural influence was primarily conveyed through church activities (Benedictines, Cistercians, Franciscans, Dominicans), and also through the strong European feudal order.

In the first half of the second millennium Croats were culturally linked with the European intellectual sphere and with Latin ecumenism, but they were also a European exception in their persistent retention of their own ethnic traditions and in the use and affirmation of the vernacular and the Croatian Glagolitic alphabet. These were ardently preserved in part of the liturgy, in a series of documents (the Baška Tablet, Istarski razvod, Vinodol Codex), in the publication of Glagolitic codices (*Novak's Missal, Hrvoje's Missal*), in Glagolitic incunabula (1483), in the Glagolitic printing house in Senj (1494), in the Glagolitic printing house in Rijeka, in Glagolitic scriptoria in Roč, Draguć, Vrtnik and elsewhere. The Croatian culture of that period also included European figures like Herman Dalmatinac (from Istria, 12th century), Priest Mikula from Gologorica (13th-14th century) or Vincent of Kastav (15th century). The name of Croatia was recorded for the first time on Idrizi's (Arabic) map (12th century).

Strong urban centres developed in an environment of widespread national cultural traditions, and through them the new European cultural influence spread into the region. In the period from the 11th to the 14th century the old coastal urban communes were these spiritual and cultural centres, and in the period from the 13th to the 15th century they were the new free towns in continental Croatia. This was the time of the complete affirmation of scholastic thought and of the Romanesque and Gothic culture and style in architecture and art.

At that time the cultural and social life of Croats equalled cultural currents in Europe. This is evidenced by the continuous development of urban life, the construction of defence walls and of fine Romanesque and Gothic buildings (mansions, cathedrals) in coastal towns (Poreč, Pula, Krk, Rab, Senj, Zadar, Šibenik, Trogir, Split, Hvar, Korčula, Dubrovnik), the development of new towns protected by walls and towers, and in the construction of predominantly Gothic sacral buildings in the towns and country of the whole continental region (Zagreb-Kaptol and Gradec, Varaždin, Krapina, Samobor, Požega, Rudine, Rijeka, Đakovo, Vukovar, Brod, Virovitica, Lepoglava). To this circle of culture and art belong the sculptures on the portal of Trogir Cathedral and the head from the former abbey church in Rudine, the cycle of frescoes in small Istrian churches and in Ston, Marija Gorska, Kalnik and Požega, and the codices written in monastery scriptoria (*Osor Evangelistary*).

Various forms of indigenous temporal and church administration developed in these urban centres, which was often active in the field of security (building town walls, towers, fortified monasteries and churches), culture (literacy, scriptoria, schools, libraries), social welfare (granaries, alms houses, pharmacies, lazarettos) and art.

Traditional cultural elements were manifested in the communal and family life of the country people and they are an important document of the Croatian culture and proof of its identity within the European sphere of that time (customs, costumes, legalized concepts of clan and joint family life, the way in which settlements and homes were built, types of work and farms, celebrations, songs, dances, oral tradition, archaic dialects, art expression, ornamentation). Original indigenous derivatives of medieval cultural currents emerged in the country, expressed through the life of many folk fraternities and village parishes and communes (with elected elders). The semi-urbanized settlements and country dwellings, and especially the hundreds of folk churches with details in the Romanesque and Gothic styles, often adorned by local masters and linked to numerous donations, with inscriptions and Glagolitic letters, are part of the indigenous Croatian culture. To that cultural circle belong brotherhood and guild rules and customs, passion plays and traditional church, family, holiday and feast customs, the wider links between regions at important fairs and their many accompanying events. All this illustrates the cultural atmosphere of Croatian towns, villages and hamlets.

Humanism, Renaissance and Baroque. The great turning point in which medieval thought and culture, enriched by traditions of the classical Hellenistic cultural circle and inspired by new thoughts of its humanist protagonists, were transformed into new humanistic cultural concepts, brought new currents into Croatian lands.

In the middle of the second millennium Croatia's cultural profile was marked by the persistent use of the Croatian language and the Glagolitic alphabet (in Istria and the northern part of the Adritic coast), and also by the intense activities of Croatian Latinists who maintained the noble traditions of classical culture in southern urban communes and in the free towns of north Croatia.

The ancestral force of the vernacular, impressed in the consciousness of the Croatian people through thousands of years of tradition, was historically affirmed in the literary and theoretic work of M. Marulić and B. Kašić. Free humanistic thought in philosophy and science showed in the work of Ivan Vitez, Ivan Česmički, F. Petrišević, A. Vrančić, I. Belostenec, A. Vramec, M. Vlačić, I. Lucić, P. Ritter-Vitezović, F. Petrić, M. Getaldić, R. Bošković and many other great men. At the same time great masters appeared in the fields of architecture and art, like J. Dalmatinac, M. Andrijić, A. Aleši, Matej of Pula, Vincent of Kastav, Blaž of Trogir, I. Pribislavić, Anton of Kaščerga, F. and L. Vranjanin, I. Duknović, P. Miličević, N. Božidarević, J. Čulinović, F. E. Robba, I. Ranger and many others. Outstanding in the field of music were I. Lukačić, I. M. Jarnović, L. Sorkočević and A. Ivančić.

Some renowned thinkers and scholars from the Croatian cultural circle worked outside their homeland and gave a great contribution to European culture, science and art. These included I. Česmički, F. and L. Vranjanin, J. Dalmatinac, I. Pribislavić, M. Vlačić, J. Klović, R. Bošković and J. Križanić.

However, in the period when urban centres were flourishing and gaining overall affirmation and when social, political and economic life reached new heights, at the time when humanistic thought and creativity were spreading through the Croatian cultural environment, the spectre of Turkish invasion rose over Croatia. From the end of the fifteenth century (the battle on Krbava Field in 1493), throughout the whole sixteenth century (the victory over the Turks at Sisak in 1593) to the end of the seventeenth century (the victorious peace treaty in Srijemski Karlovci in 1699), Croatia was exposed to the worst kind of hardship and was in danger of complete destruction. This was the time when Turkish invasion and Venetian, Austrian and Hungarian encroachment turned life in Croatia into a fight for survival.

In the sixteenth and seventeenth centuries the intensity of cultural life persisted in literature and art, in architecture and education (grammar schools, university studies – in Lepoglava, Zagreb, Varaždin, Poreč, Zadar, Split, Dubrovnik), in the remaining free continental area, called the *reliquiae reliquiarum,* and in Istria and the coastal town communes. This was the circle from which čakavian and kajkavian cultural folk traditions emanated, parallel with the activities of Glagolitic literary and printing commuties, a high humanistic awareness expressed in the poetry and art of the Dalmatian area, and strong kajkavian creativity in northern regions. After the liberation of Slavonia, under new historic conditions in the eighteenth century, intense cultural life developed in the vast Slavonian štokavian region, too.

In this harsh period of Croatian history the unbreakable force of creativity came to expression in the new baroque style in town planning and architecture (Varaždin, Zagreb, Osijek-Tvrđa, Požega, Poreč, Rijeka, Zadar, Šibenik, Split, Hvar, Dubrovnik), and in art (Lepoglava, Zagreb, Split, Dubrovik). Summer-houses in the Renaissance tradition were built in the Dubrovnik area and on the Elafiti islands, Dubrovnik was renewed (after the 1667 earthquake), patricians and sea captains built mansions along the coast (Split, Zadar, Poreč, Rijeka), baroque mansions, villas and manors were built in the free continental region (Varaždin, Zagreb, Križevci, the Zagorje countryside), and in newly-liberated Slavonia (Osijek-Tvrđa, Vukovar, Požega, Našice, Đakovo, Daruvar, Virovitica). In the baroque period the same creative force was felt in the construction of sacral buildings (Dubrovnik, Hvar, Rijeka, Varaždin, Trški vrh, Belec, Zagreb, Bjelovar, Osijek, Brod, Vinkovci).

The Modern Age. The overall transformation of social and political life that the French Revolution initiated in part of Europe overthrew the feudal society and gave rise to a new social order and the middle class. In Croatia awakening consciousness about an age-old ethnic identity resulted in the Illyrian Movement and the Croatian National Revival, which based insight about the glorious past of the Croatian people on authentic sources from Croatian history, archaeological finds and the traditions of Croatian cultural identity. Great men, revivalists and fighters for national rights (J. Drašković, Lj. Gaj, I. Kukuljević-Sakcinski, J. Jelačić, J. J. Strossmayer, I. Mažuranić), worked on spriritual renewal and struggled for political freedom and for the recognition of Croatian statehood. They initiated the foundation of new and renewed existing cultural, scholarly, art and educational institutions with the purpose of strengthening the moral and scientific foundations of the Croatian people's political struggle for their ancient rights.

At that time communications and economic ties linked Croatia more strongly with Europe, and the Croatian language was affirmed in schools, parliament and in the theatre.

The revival had a strong reflection in Croatia's public, scientific, art and cultural life in the second half of the nineteenth and in the twentieth century.

This was a period when European heights were reached in Croatia in the humanities and in scientific research. These activities were carried out in the Academy, at universities, in scholarly libraries, in important archives, in rich museums and galleries, in scientific research institutes, in cultural institutions, in theatres, schools and at many conferences, performances, festivals, concerts and exhibitions.

The high level of scientific achievement, cultural accomplishment and artistic expression attained in Croatia to date ensures its honourable place in European thought, culture and civilization. In an atmosphere of freedom the Croatian cultural identity of the Croatian people will be affirmed even more clearly on the wide international scene.

Andre MOHOROVIČIĆ

THE CROATIAN HERITAGE OF FINE ARTS
WITHIN THE EUROPEAN CULTURAL TRADITION

We shall attempt to answer the question of whether the artistic monuments in Croatia are simply the result of absorption – the spread and acceptance of art forms that originated and developed in other cultural centres, thereby merely adding quantitatively to the European artistic heritage, or whether art in Croatia has made a qualitative, creative contribution to it. The cultural heritage on the territory of Croatia, in our view, includes works which belong to the treasury of European art, and without which certain chapters of European art history are incomplete. It should be mentioned, however, that many of these are unknown as such to the public abroad, and have not received general recognition, since they are not included in major surveys and summaries of European art made to date. The reason for this is not the unimportance of these works nor their inferior artistic quality, but lack of information. The authors of surveys of European and world art are often, unfortunately, too little acquainted with art monuments in Croatia. Still less are they able (because of the language barrier) to follow the growing number of scholarly studies published in recent decades interpreting these monuments in line with the principles of contemporary scholarship. Finally, there is the fact that some of the major monuments in Croatia have only lately been thoroughly studied and properly interpreted. To illustrate our point, we shall mention here just a few of the more important monuments in Croatia of European significance.

From the prehistoric period there are some specific regional forms of artifacts, for instance, the incrusted Vučedol pottery.

In the Roman age there is Diocletian's Palace (4th century), one of the most important extant examples of the architecture of late antiquity, combining the diverse artistic influences of the vast empire. The monumental imperial palace was adapted during later centuries into the small medieval city of Split.

The sacral buildings of Salona occupy an essential place in the art history of the Early-Christian period (4th-6th century), having supplied the evidence for propounding and checking theories on some of the central problems concerning the architecture of the period (e. g. the origin of the Christian basilica) and other questions of a cultural nature (the relationship between the official and the martyr cult or the »twin« basilicas).

From the »golden age« of Byzantine art in the reign of Justinian I, we have the episcopal complex and mosaics of Poreč (6th century), whose iconographic originality and exceptional artistic quality long ago led to comparison with the contemporary, and better known, mosaics of Ravenna.

Following the settlement of the Slavs in the 7th century, the period of the independent Croatian state (9th-11th century) saw the development of Pre-Romanesque architecture (»Early-Croatian«) – small churches with diverse ground-plans and shapes, which have been preserved or whose remains have been discovered in a relatively large number (about one hundred), not only compared with the buildings of other South Slav peoples in that period, but in relation to the architectural heritage of other European nations. These churches form a separate group of buildings over which art historians and other scholars have crossed swords, debating the crucial question of whether Roman antiquity or so-called »barbarian« art played the vital role in the formation of early medieval architecture: the theories of continuity and discontinuity in culture.

In contrast with these small structures, the huge rotunda of St Donatus in Zadar (9th century) with its ambulatory on the upper floor and three apses, ranks among the most imposing Pre-Romanesque churches of centralised type in Europe. A distinctive group from this period is made up of churches with massive rounded counterforts and a bell-tower in the middle of the facade, such as St Saviour's (Sveti Spas) on the Cetina (11th century). Marking a crucial moment in the birth of Romanesque architectural sculpture, they are unique monuments of the transistion from the Pre-Romanesque age, when ornament completely dominated reliefs for four hundred years, to the early Romanesque, when the human image and figural compositions reappeared.

The Pre-Romanesque and early Romanesque plaitwork reliefs, structurally linked with the buildings of the Early-Croatian period, have already been accorded a niche in the treasury of world art. A. Malraux included the stone plaques from from the church of St Domenica in Zadar with their plaitwork, linear and low-relief figural compositions of the life of Christ (11th century) in his Musée imaginaire. The cross-ribbed vault in the bell tower of the Benedictine Monastery in Zadar (1105) is one of the oldest reliably dated in Europe, while the portal of Trogir Cathedral by Master Radovan (1240) is the most outstanding work of medieval sculpture not only in Yugoslavia but in this part of Europe.

Cult vessel in the shape of a stylized dove, the most famous find of the Vučedol culture, 2800–2500 BC, Archaeological Museum in Zagreb

Tripartite vessel with indented ornament – Sarvaš, Slavonia, Archaeological Museum in Zagreb

Vučedol – model of a baker's oven – 2800–2500 BC, Archaeological Museum in Zagreb

Vučedol – large dish. 2800–2500 BC, Archaeological Museum in Zagreb

Sacrificial vessel from Dalj, Slavonia, 7th c. BC, Archaeological Museum in Zagreb

Juraj Dalmatinac (George of Dalmatia), master of the transitional or »mixed« Gothic-Renaissance style, made his contribution to the development of early Renaissance sculpture, and by the implementation of an original assembly method using stone slabs in the construction of Šibenik Cathedral (1441–1473) made it possible to build a unique structure exclusively of stone from its foundations to the roof vaulting and the top of the dome, without recourse to any other materials.

Juraj's successor, the Renaissance architect and sculptor Nikola Firentinac (Nicholas the Florentine, 1475–1505), continued the building of Šibenik Cathedral, creating the first and only functional and organic Renaissance facade in Europe in which the »trefoil« shape of the gable corresponds to the shape of the interior vaulting. Nikola Firentinac was responsible, with A. Aleši, for the Renaissance chapel of the Blessed John in Trogir (1468–1482), also entirely of stone, influenced by Juraj and local classical tradition (the Small Temple of Diocletian's Palace). With the new relationship of sculpture and architecture and his unprecedented use of monumental sculpture, Nikola applied a method which was to be further developed in European art in the next century, in the age of the high Renaissance.

The third original creation of the Renaissance period in Croatia – besides Šibenik Cathedral and the Trogir chapel – are the Renaissance summer villas of the 15th and 16th centuries raised by local builders for the Dubrovnik patricians on the territory of the free Dubrovnik Republic.

In type and quality, in their asymmetrical ground-plans, functional organization of space and relationship to their natural surroundings, these have no adequate counterparts in contemporary European architecture.

Finally, the artistic heritage of Croatia abounds in entities whose value lies in their organic fusion of monuments from various periods in various styles. These are the towns – syntheses of works of art created by many generations in different ages: Split, where every epoch since antiquity has left its traces; the Renaissance »ideal« town of Karlovac (1579) in the shape of a six-pointed star; Gothic-Renaissance-baroque Dubrovnik; Roman-Romanesque Zadar; the 14th century planned Gothic towns of Veliki Ston and Mali Ston; the Renaissance isle of Šipan, and others.

Works of art are the traces of time in space. Looking back from our present standpoint at the perspective of bygone centuries of continuous creativity on the territory of Croatia, we can perceive a division into two essentially different epochs; that of the pre-Slav civilisations and cultures, and the period from the Slav settlement in the 7th century to the present day. Just as those pre-Slav civilisations, above all the Roman, not only left an indelible imprint with their surviving monuments, but also influenced our creative spirits in the past, so the entire artistic heritage of Croatia forms part of our culture today. Provided, of course, that we are acquainted with it. It is hoped that this book may serve to further such an acquaintance.

Radovan Ivančević

Roman gold coins, 1st c., Archaeological Museum in Zagreb

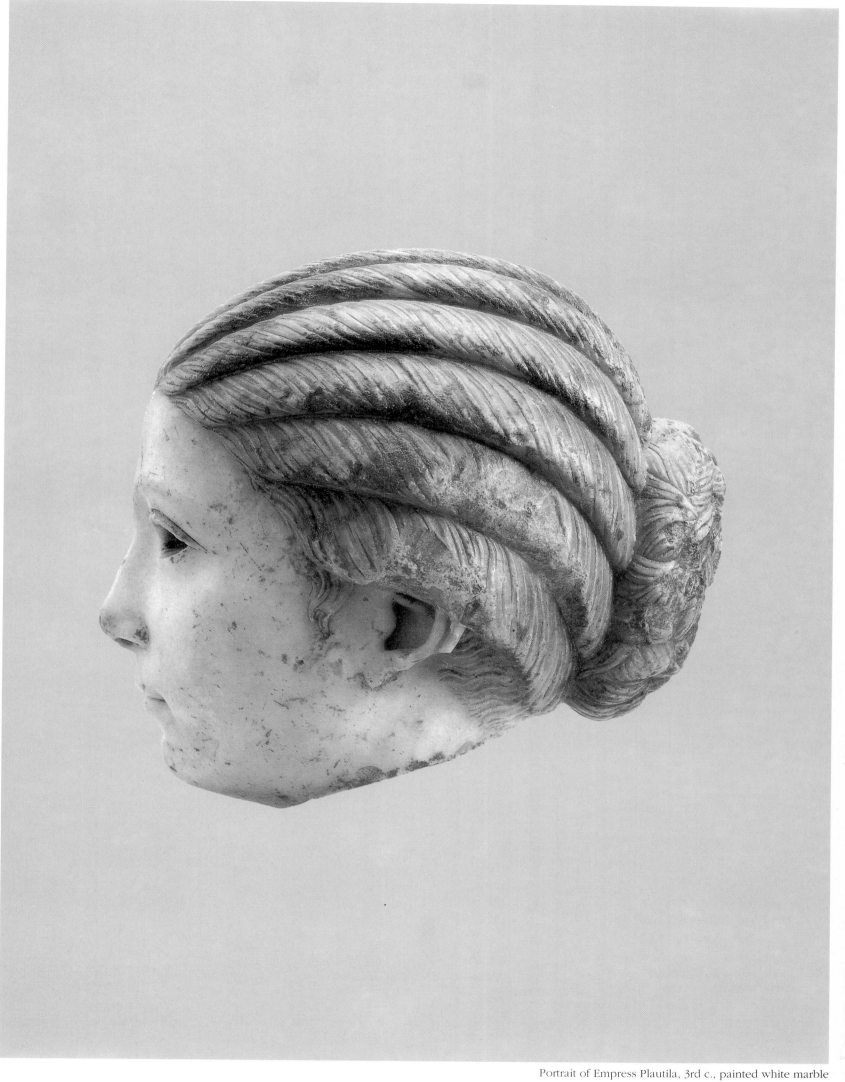

Portrait of Empress Plautila, 3rd c., painted white marble

Peristyle of Diocletian's Palace in Split

Ruins of Salona (amphitheatre), one of the largest excavation sites of Roman and Early-Christian culture

The Basilica of Euphrasius in Poreč. Outstanding among Early-Christian structures is the Basilica of Euphrasius adroned with mosaics on the level of those in Ravenna

Figure of a Croatian ruler from the 10—11th c., baptistery of Split Cathedral

Zadar, church of St Donatus, the most monumental medieval building in Croatia. It was built by Bishop Donatus of Zadar

Andrija Buvina, two panels from the door of Split Cathedral, *Laying Jesus in the Tomb* and *The Last Supper*. Master Buvina made this wooden door in 1214. It consists of 28 reliefs from the Life of Christ.

Trogir, portal of the Cathedral of St. Laurence, world masterpiece of Romanesque sculpture by Master Radovan, 1240

Blaž Jurjev, *Imago pietatis and saints,* All Saints Church in Korčula. Blaž Jurjev (1375–1450) was the greatest Croatian Gothic painter.

Beram, *Flight into Egypt,* one of the most beautiful frescos in Istria and Croatia. Vincent of Kastav painted the graveyard church of St Mary on the Rocks.

Juraj Dalmatinac, *The Flagellation* (1448). Relief on the altar of Split Cathedral, the finest sculpture by Juraj Dalmatinac, builder of Šibenik Cathedral. Early-Renaissance.

Dubrovnik, cloister of the Franciscan Monastery, built at the beginning of the 14th c. in the Romanesque-Gothic style

Dubrovnik, Renaissance Sorkočević summer house

Ivan Ranger, important baroque painter, Pauline. Painted fine illusionist frescos in many churches in Croatia: in Belec, the ceiling of the old pharmacy in the Franciscan Monastery in Varaždin, St Mary's in Lepoglava, the baroque St John's chapel in Gorica, the baroque St George's chapel in Purga, St Jerome's in Štrigova

St Catherine's church in Zagreb, newly-restored interior: stucco work, main altar, side altars and pulpit

THE RICHNESS AND BEAUTY OF CROATIAN NATIONAL COSTUME

Beauty and variety of landscape, rich diversity of plant and animal life, widely differing climatic conditions – all these are part of the attraction of Croatia. And this diversity is reflected in the works that men and women have created, especially the Croats as the most numerous inhabitants at the region.

Folk creativity finds visual expression in articles of everyday use, and many ancient craft traditions were cherished down until the middle of the present century, some of them showing traces of several thousand of years of unbroken application.

Among the traditional crafts a special place is taken by the making of national costume, both those garments that people wore everyday and those that they wore for special occasions. The varied forms that such clothing took in different regions was determined by a number of factors; natural conditions, the economic position of individuals and of the region, contacts with the outside world, and the great cultural and historical events which affected certain regions.

Croatia's stormy history, caught between East and West, plus regional variation, were the basic forming factors of Croatian folk art and costume. The regional variations ranged from the ferile lowlands of the north;

the rocky mountains dividing these from the coast; and the coast itself: part mountain, part sea and islands.

But even in this variety we can discern a coherent linkage with the ancient Mediterranean and the old Balkan past. There is a Roman and a Slav/Croat heritage, later enriched by Gothic, Renaissance, baroque and in some parts by Turkish/Oriental elements.

The wonderful variety of Croatian costume can be seen to fall into three large groups: Pannonian, Dinaric and Adriatic. Each of these has common elements.

The Pannonian region lies between the Drava, the Kupa and the Sava. The main occupation is agriculture and the costumes of both men and women are basically made of white linen which women wove themselves to meet their own needs.

Men's clothing is similar throughout the region: wide, white linen trousers with a white linen shirt worn over them. Narrow cloth trousers for winter wear were taken over from military uniform. Tailor-made clothing or fur jackets completed the costume. A fur cap or black hat was also worn. Both men and women wore wide leather sandals (*opanci*) or sometimes boots.

The women's costume was more varied. The extreme north-west part of the region showed considerable variety. South of the Sava the linen had richly

Folk group from Posavina

Folk costume from Šestine, Zagreb

woven patterning. Posavina (Sava valley) costume was found the length of the Sava from Zagreb to Jasenovac, made of very fine homespun linen. For special occasions and important holidays girls, especially brides, would wear skirts, blouses and aprons all rich with a red woven pattern. A feature of this region was the girl's head-covering which was a kind of crown worn with silk ribbons. Married women wore a little cap and a scarf, often woven with a silk pattern and worn in a great variety of ways. Further east in Slavonia women's costume was originally a long tunic which later developed into blouse and skirt. This was decorated on the sleeves and the back of the skirt with embroidered bands in red, blue or black cotton. With these a fringed, woollen apron was worn, and for festive occasions was decoratively woven. The most elaborate specimens were beautified with gold-thread embroidery and with them went a silk apron, shawl and headscarf also embroidered with gold or silver thread. At the northeastern end of the Pannonian region is Baranja where a different variant was worn, similar to that of Slavonia in its basic use of linen, but with woven woollen apron worn over the skirt. Besides horizontal lines in geometric or flower patterns here they also wove animal forms, especially birds, which still today are executed with great skill by the women of these parts.

Girl in old folk costume from Bizovac in Podravska Slavonia

Folklore Festival in Zagreb in 1994

Old man from the Imotska krajina region

Natural and artificial flowers, silk ribbons, sparkling sequins, tiny glass beads, necklaces of coral, mother-of-pearl or glass beads, jingling chains of gold or silver coins were an essential part of the dress of young women and girls, especially coming to expression in wedding clothing. It is in the Pannonian region that most of the truly ancient Slav characteristics have been preserved, those that are also found among other Slav nations.

From the northern plains almost to the shores of the Adriatic stretches the mountainous Dinaric region, the southern and eastern parts of which are in Croatia. The traditional way of life was based on sheep and wool is

the most important element of the national costume of men and women alike.

Men's tousers here were blue or brown, long and narrow in the western parts, wider and more oriental in style, reaching just below the knee in the eastern. Above them was worn a sleeveless waistcoat and a short jacket. With these, on festive occasions, weapons were worn, especially a pistol or knife tucked into a wide leather belt. The most highly prized waistcoats were studded with silver studs. The origin of these waistcoats was very ancient and they have been found in archaeological sites in the region. Traditional head-wear was a round red cap with tassels on the edge, and this element has been longest preserved.

Shieldbearer in *Alka* procession, Sinj

Bagpipe player from Dalmatia

On their feet both men and women wore several layers of woollen or cloth stockings, variously decorated, and sandals with soft leather soles, the uppers of braided stringwork. This was the normal footwear of the whole Dinaric region.

Women's costume consisted of several layers. Next to the skin came a long linen tunic with open sleeves decorated with cross-stitch embroidery. The same embroidery was used round the neck and on the edges of the front opening. This tunic was girdled with a long woven belt, in front a fringed woollen apron with geometric woven patterns. Over the tunic a fairly long, sleeveless woollen coat was worn and under it, in win-

Women from Sinj in old folk costume

Girl in the folk costume of the Makarska coast.

Folk costume from Ravni Kotari, surroundings of Zadar

Istrian folk costume from central Istria, near Žminj

Istria, *roženice* players (a characteristic Istrian folk instrument)

ter, a dress with sleeves. This dress was white for girls and called *bilaca* (white) while for women it was blue and called *modrina* (blue). The cloth parts would be edged with bright, coloured braid with very finely executed tiny patterns.

Unmarried girls wore red caps and married women white scarves. In the Vrlika costume a white scarf worn over a red cap meant a girl looking for a husband. Around Zadar the scarf, like the tunic, was richly embroidered in silk, and silken embroidery was also part of the Konavle costume near Dubrovnik.

Folk costume from the island of Krk

Abundant silver trimmings were worn especially on the head and round the neck: brooches, pins, buckles, ear-rings, and necklaces. Money, sometimes large quantities, would be sewn onto clothing. In the Vrlika costume girls would wear a large cloth band with money sewn on to it which was sometimes their dowry.

Some of the elements and the embellishments of the national costume of these parts is very ancient in origin. This is understandable since the way of life hardly changed from ancient times until this century. It was largely based on semi-nomadic sheep rearing.

The Adriatic region includes the coastal strip and the islands. Life developed under the influence of Medi-

terranean history and economic and cultural developments. Any specific national costume began to be lost during the first half of the nineteenth century. Nevertheless in some places, traditional costume could be found even between the wars.

Men's costume was distinguished by wide, woollen, baggy trousers and a blue, knitted stocking-shaped cap, the tip falling towards the shouders. This remained longest on the island of Krk, but can be found here and there on other islands. But the Dinaric costume was widespread in the region also because of the large numbers of highlanders who fled to the coast to escape from the Turks in the fifteenth and sixteenth centuries.

Dancers from Orlec, island of Cres

A girl from the island of Susak

There are several variants of women's costume. Typical of them all is the fact that the original, simple, long tunic was topped by a home-spun woolen skirt. Straight, stiff folds were also typical of the women's clothing which showed two basic variants. In one the long pleats were gathered onto a bodice and were left open at the sides. In the other the pleats were sewn onto a sleeveless blouse which had a long v-shaped opening showing the tunic below. These, together with accentuated waist, were Renaissance characteristics. In some places late baroque also influenced women's clothes and the bodice became a tight corslet. Earlier tunics and headscarves had been embroidered in colour, but from the Renaissance white became the

Old folk costumes from the town of Pag

fashion and the use of lace began, the finest that which was part of the costume of the island of Pag, and Pag lace is still famous.

On the head a square, white head-scarf was worn in some parts, and in others a long white scarf was wound around the head. This is one of the items of dress that was part of the old Slav tradition.

Coral, mother-of-pearl and silver accessories were common and also gold ornaments made by local master-craftsmen. Many ornaments were filigree work sometimes incorporating pearls or semi-precious stones.

The costume of the Adriatic region presented a very varied picture and sometimes very ancient elements would be combined with quite recent ones. The coast had always been open to outside influences and fundamentally affected by historical change. All these things were reflected in costume.

Croatian national costume may be thought of as a kind of book from which can be read the stormy past of the people who lived in these parts.

Jelka Radauš Ribarić

44

Girls from Blato on Korčula at the Folklore Festival
in Zagreb, 1994

Women's costume from Konavle near Dubrovnik

Participants in the Folklore Festival beside Manduševac Well on Ban Jelačić Square in Zagreb

International Folklore Festival in Zagreb, the most interesting festival of the kind in Europe.

Roe-buck and does in winter, Risnjak National Park

OUR LOVELY CROATIA

THE CROATIAN NATURAL HERITAGE

The natural features and beauty of Croatia are much greater than the country's small size would suggest. Croatia has plains, mountains and coast, it is both a maritime and a continental country, which accounts for its natural variety and richness. This becomes more understandable when we remember that Croatia is also a country with a wealth of varied karst phenomena, and that its shoreline, one of the most indented in the world, is 5,835 kilometres long and has 718 islands.

Croatia's natural beauty is reflected in the legislation enacted to protect some areas, localities, plant and animal species. This protection, which complies with all international criteria, covers about 7 per cent of Croatia. There are 7 national parks, 6 nature parks, ·71 scientific reserves, 72 monuments of nature, 28 landscapes, 23 forest parks, 114 monuments of park architecture, 380 animal and 44 plant species. Some of these areas and species can be found on international lists of reserves and imperilled species, compiled for various conventions and scientific programmes.

Lonjsko polje

The river Lonja

Spoonbills

Orahovica, remains of medieval Ružica on the slopes of forested Papuk

East Croatia is part of the vast Panonnian Plain whose prevailing natural characteristics are oak forests, fluvial and fluvial-marsh biotopes along the Sava, Drava and Danube rivers, and a rich animal life. Slavonian hills, the result of palaeozoic folding, also contribute to the appearance of this region. The Kopački rit and Lonjsko polje Nature Parks fittingly represent the fluvial-marsh area, and the planned Papuk Nature Park will represent the mountain biotopes and landscapes.

Its rich plant and animal life make Kopački rit one of the most beautiful nature parks. 267 bird species have been recorded in this pocket edged by the Drava and the Danube, many of them with a great number of specimens. Deer, wild boar, marten and wild cat also inhabit the forests of Kopački rit. The central and most important part of the nature park is protected as a zoological reserve.

Lonjsko polje Nature Park covers the floodland between Sisak and Nova Gradiška in the river-basins of the Sava, Lonja and Struga, 500 square kilometres of water channels, marshes, water meadows and forests. 236 bird species have been recorded, 130 of which nest there. Many of them can be found on the world list of endangered species. There are many villages along the river Sava and its channels. Their houses are wood, of interesting and elaborate architecture, and the storks nesting on the roofs complete the impression of a harmonious bond between man and nature (the village of Čigoč was recently proclaimed a European Stork Village).

Papuk is the most important mountain range of Slavonia, with uniform and well preserved forests important in the ecological balance of this part of Croatia. Papuk is also of geological interest because it is built of eruptive, metamorphic and carbonate rocks.

Central Croatia has a heterogeneous landscape. Several mountain ranges about 1000 metres high rise from the gentle hills covering the sediments of what was once the Pannonian Sea: Žumberak, Medvednica and Ivančica. Forested Medvednica and Ivančica rise from the sur-

Hedgehog

Yellow water lily

View of Zagorje and Medvednica from the Gubec Monument in Stubica

Thick forests and marshes near Trakošćan

Sošice, in the heart of picturesque Žumberak

The bottom tranquill course of the Mrežnica

rounding agricultural countryside. Žumberak and the Sa-mobor hills are an interesting combination of forests, open meadows and pastures with hill villages. Medvednica was proclaimed a nature park in 1981 because of its well preserved and varied forests and because of its overall importance for Zagreb. Žumberak is to be proclaimed a nature park soon.

Two more regions, very different from the previous ones and from each other, are planned as future nature parks. The first, between Trakošćan, Macelj and Ravna gora, is a typical picturesque landscape of Croatian Zagorje, with vineyards, cultural and historic monuments and recording the overall presence of man. The second region is the river Mrežnica, whose natural features make it the most interesting river of the Kupa basin. The Kupa basin has four main rivers: the Kupa, the Dobra, the Mrežnica and the Korana. They flow from the south and west through a region of low and »shallow« karst, and mark this part of central Croatia. Typical and strong karst springs, often picturesque river gorges and rich plant and animal life, are only some of the qualities of these beautiful crystalline rivers. One of them, the Dobra, temporarily disappears down a magnificent swallow-hole (Đulin ponor in Ogulin), and the Mrežnica is a continuation of streams that percolated through the mountain hinterland. Numerous travertine cascades have turned its course into a series of small lakes, sometimes in rocky gorges, sometimes among green woods and meadows.

Following the course of these rivers upstream, we reach the mountains. This part of Croatia consists of two historical and geographical districts: Gorski Kotar and Lika.

Capercaille

Starling

Hoopoe

Lanner

Sparrow-hawk

Dark-breasted barn own

Risnjak National Park, a mountain in Gorski Kotar with a rich plant and animal life

Gorski Kotar is the most forested region of Croatia (60 per cent of its territory is under forests), and these well preserved forests and outstanding relief give the main stamp to its nature and landscape. Risnjak National Park was founded because of the forests, because almost all forest communities are represented here on a relatively small area in the range from 700 to 1500 metres above sea level. Elsewhere the forest communities are widely dispersed. Risnjak is a national park of great scientific importance.

However, Risnjak is not the only reserve important for foresters and botanists. Bijele stijene and Samarske stijene in the central part of the Velika Kapela mountain chain are just as important. Here a great wealth of white stone sculptures – towers, cones, domes – a real geomorphological collection, competes with the magnificence of the virgin forests. Another of the interesting reliefs of Gorski Kotar is Mount Klek, the advance-guard of the Gorski Kotar mountains, an outstanding accent in the landscape of the Ogulin basin and one of the mountaineering and rock-climbing legends of Croatia. Klek's plant life has qualified it as a botanical reserve.

The forests of Gorski Kotar often depend on relief, and relief and waterways are interconnected and mutually conditioned. This well-known fact is most impressively illustrated below Skrad, where a mountain stream has cut a deep gorge through the limestone, in places only several meters wide (»The Devil's Passage«). A path for visitors, hazardous at first sight, has been cut through it. The hydrographic phenomena of Gorski Kotar include the source of the Kupa, one of the biggest and most beautiful springs in Croatia.

View from the top of Risnjak

Lynx on Risnjak

Bijele stijene (White Rocks) on Risnjak

Dormouse

Fox

Pine marten

Unlike mountainous Gorski Kotar, the landscape of Lika includes spacious poljes, karst plateaus (Ličko polje, Gacko polje and Krbavsko polje are the largest), which are of equal important in the landscape. Their altitude is over 500 meters (only Gacko polje is somewhat lower), so Lika has every right to be included in the mountain region. Lika is edged by the great mountain ranges of Velebit, Lička Plješivica and Kapela, making it an isolated and separate natural entity.

Croatia's biggest underground rivers, the Lika and the Gacka, run through Lika. Caves and swallow-holes are regular features of the karst, and underground rivers of this size give Lika a special mark. One of them, the Gacka, is also one of the best-known trout-waters in Europe.

On the eastern edge of Lika, where Mala Kapela and Lička Plješivica meet, stretches a pearl of the Croatian karst – the Plitvice Lakes. A sequence of 16 lakes, some of them in forests and some in a gorge, are interconnected by many large and small cascades. The height difference between the highest and the lowest lake is 134 metres. The cascades and lakes result from active biodynamic processes in the carbonate rocks, as the water dissolves the limestone and then deposits it on the cascades in the form of fragile travertine. The present cascades are no older than 4,000 years, and some of them have grown over two metres in the last hundred years. Although there had been hopes of proclaiming the area a national park in 1914, this was not realized until 1949. In 1979 the Plitvice Lakes were included in UNESCO's list of the World Natural Heritage.

Mount Velebit, a mountain 150 kilometres long, rises like a huge rampart from the west edge of Lika's plateaus.

Cerovačke špilje caves

The foaming silver waters of the Plitvice Lakes

The brown bear, a permanent inhabitant of Lika and Gorski Kotar

A brown bear in front of its den, Risnjak National Park

Bear cubs beside the River Kupa

Velebit, the most important mountain in Croatia, stretches for 145 km along the Adriatic Sea. A UNESCO charter includes it in the International Network of Biosphere Reserves.

People from Lika and from the coastal claim this mountain as theirs, because it faces the sea, as well. Velebit is the most important and most interesting Croatian mountain because of its great size and its natural characteristics. It is also legendary in the consciousness of the people, and was often an inspiration for patriotic poetry.

In 1949 a small part of Velebit, the deep gorges and forests of Paklenica in the south part of the mountain, on the sea side, were proclaimed a national park. In 1978 the mountain got international acknowledgement: it was included in the international network of Man and the Biosphere. Finally, in 1981, the Croatian Parliament proclaimed the whole of Velebit a nature park, covering a territory of 2000 square kilometres. The spatial plan of Croatia foresees that the top belt of the mountain will be a national park. This top belt has the richest relief and the greatest botanical importance. From Zavižan, over Rožanski kukovi and Hajdučki kukovi rocks, Kozjak and Dabri in the northern half of the mountain, to Stapina, Bojnice, Tulove grede and Prosenjak in south Velebit, stretches a treasury of weird-shaped rocks, mostly on palaeogeneous breccia. In this Velebit has no peer far outside the borders of Croatia. The wealth of surface shapes is accompanied by a wealth of »underground landscapes« in the numerous caves and pits; the best known are Cerovečke pećine near Gračac and Lukina jama in Hajdučki kukovi (over 1300 meters deep).

Botanists have recorded 2,700 plant species on Velebit, and among the many Croatian endemics, a special place belongs to a plant that is found only here, so it has been named the *Degenia velebitica*. The most interesting animals of Velebit include the brown bear (*Ursus arctos*), the wolf (*Canis lupus*), the chamois (*Rupicapra rupicapra*), the golden eagle (*Aquila chrysaetos*), the short-toed eagle (*Cyrcaetus gallicus*) and the griffin vulture (*Gyps fulvus*).

Leontopodium alpinum, edelweiss

Paklenica is a small part of Croatia's biggest mountain, Velebit. The Velika Paklenica and Mala Paklenica gorges are near the Adriatic Coast Road.

Clear streams and small rivers run through the deep gorges of Velika Paklenica

Aquilegia vulgaris – columbine

Lilium bulbiferum – lily

Helleborus macrantus – hellebore

Daphne Mesereum – spurge laurel

Deer on the meadows of Brijuni

The Croatian shoreline begins with Croatia's largest peninsula Istria in the north, its landscape dominated by Mount Učka. Učka is one of the identification marks of Istria, and also of the neighbouring Kvarner area, Rijeka and the Opatija Riviera at its foot. The eastern side of Učka has an interesting altitude profile of various forest communities, starting with the hornbeam and bay, continuing with the oak and sweet chestnut, and ending with the beech.

Another identification mark of the Istrian landscape are the old towns built on high ground. Nature dictated their proportions, and man and history harmoniously built their presence into the natural environment.

Istria's west coast has two spots of special natural interest: Lim Bay and the Brijuni Islands. Although Lim Bay looks like a fjord, its origin is different. It is breathtakingly lovely, especially for people who know that it is the flooded valley of a river that once ran there, the same river that disappears down the magnificent swallow-hole in the middle of Pazin. The bay is the winter habitat and hatching ground of many species of fish, and has been proclaimed an ichtyological reserve.

Brijuni, near Pula, are the most indented Istrian islands. The 14 islands cover a total area of 7.3 square kilometres, about three quarters of which is taken up by the largest island – Veliki (Great) Brijun. The indigenous and well-preserved Mediterranean vegetation, relatively well-preserved marine life and a first-class cultural heritage (especially Roman remains) were good reasons for proclaiming the islands and the surrounding sea a national park.

The islands in the Kvarner area are relatively large, and each of them has some feature worth mentioning in this short review of the Croatian heritage. First there is the interesting crypto-depression of Vransko jezero lake on Cres, then the griffin vulture reserves on Cres and Krk, the forest reserves of Dundo Wood on Rab and Punta Križa on Cres, the habitats of marsh birds on Pag (Veliko blato, Malo blato and Kolansko blato), and the beaches on Krk, Rab and Pag.

A special feature of this region is the sandstone island of Susak. The fine sandy sediment can be found elsewhere along the Croatian coast, but nowhere does it entirely build an island 98 metres high. The explanation lies in the last glacial period (pleistocene) when the sea level was almost a hundred metres lower, which means there was no sea around what is today the island. The winds were stronger than the ones that blow today and they could bring and deposit tiny grains of sand. The sand on Susak resulted in a specific agrarian landscape with a monoculture of vineyards, and reeds planted to protect the sandy plots from erosion.

Brijuni National Park covers an area of 36 km². It has a total of 14 islands and islets. Culturally, historically and naturally, the Brijuni are Istria's most interesting islands.

Griffin vulture from the island of Cres

Dolphins, dance above and below the sea

The Krka, »necklaces« at Roški slap fall

Visovačko jezero lake

What the rivers of the Kupa basin are in the interior, the Zrmanja, Krka, Cetina and Neretva are in the coastal region. These rivers flow through karst regions and have identical properties: strong springs, picturesque valleys, travertine cascades, clean and clear water, and the plants and animals that live in them are interesting, and often endemic. One of them, the Krka, became one of Croatia's seven national parks in 1985. Its place in this category was never under dispute, but its proclamation as an national park was put off because of parallel plans to build power plants. The cascades of the Krka originated in the same way as those of the Plitvice Lakes, but here there was much more water so the lakes are bigger (Visovac Lake) and the gorges more impressive.

Especially outstanding in the course of the Zrmanja is the magnificent gorge between Obrovac and the Novigrad Sea. The Cetina has the famous Omiška probojnica pass, Gubavica fall and several strong springs. The Neretva is a world of its own in its final course that runs through Croatia. Unlike the other Dalmatian rivers, the Neretva carried more material with it so the process of accumulation occurred faster than the sea level rose. This is how the beautiful landscape of the alluvium plain developed, with marshes in places, out of which jut little limestone islands

The Krka is the most spectacular and most beautiful river of the Croatian karst. The greater part of the 72 km long river runs through gorges. It has large branching cascades, and Skradinski Buk is 46 m high and has seventeen levels.

The Biokovo range of unique beauty streches for 50 km along the sea

of the earlier relief. This type of rich fluvial biotope was ideal for the life of marsh birds, which gave the lower Neretva, together with Kopački rit and Lonjsko polje, a place in international lists of similar localities (Ramsar Convention).

Mount Biokovo stretches along the coast between the Cetina and the Neretva. Nowhere in Croatia do such high (up to 1500 metres) and rocky mountain crags approach so close to the sea as they do here. While Velebit is a collection of phenomena, Biokovo and its foot form an unrepeatable landscape. The gorgeous beaches of the Makarska Riviera are a gift of the mountain. Here torrents crumbled the rocks and carried them to the sea, which tamed them shaping the beaches of today.

Biokovo's hinterland is no less interesting. Behind it stretches the Imotska krajina region with its well-known lakes (Crveno jezero, Modro jezero and a few smaller ones). Their shapes, sizes, and above all their origin are unique; the lakes were formed in enormous underground hollows whose ceilings caved in during an earthquake. The bed of Modro jezero (Blue Lake) has estavells (springs during the rainy period, swallow-holes when it is dry), so the water level varies up to 70 metres. Crveno jezero (Red Lake) is a real marvel of the karst: a precipice, a »well« 500 metres deep with a diameter of about 200 metres! Over half of this depth is filled with water!

The Dalmatian islands compete in magnificence with the coastline. Foremost is the most indented group of

Chamois

Modro jezero lake and the Imotski plateau

The Kornati Islands, the most intended group of islands in the European Mediterranean. Kornati National Park covers 224 km². Many clifs are up to 100 m high. The sea around Kornati is rich in marine life.

Telašćica, Dugi otok

Mediterranean islands – the Kornati. Perhaps we should say the densest group, because 140 islands, islets and cliffs (a total of 69 square kilometres) spread over an area of about 300 square kilometres. A labyrinth of rock and sea! The boundaries of the national park include the surrounding sea as an equal segment because the marine life here is considered one of the richest and most diverse in the Mediterranean. On the neighbouring island of Dugi Otok, Telašćica Nature Park continues onto the Kornati National Park. It features one of the most indented bays and the highest cliffs of the Croatian coastline (vertical cliffs up to 200 metres high).

Almost all the central-Dalmatian islands have something of interest to offer, sometimes bizarre. On Brač this is the Zlatni rat (Golden Point) beach that juts out into the sea like a tongue, its end shifting depending on the direction of the wind. Hvar harbour is protected by the magnificently indented islands of Pakleni otoci. Vis has the bizarre bay of Stiniva, Biševo the famous Modra špilja (Blue Grotto). In the open sea there are two small volcanic islands, Brusnik and Jabuka, the only ones of their kind in Croatia (all other islands are built of rock sediments: limestone, dolomite and flysh).

The Neretva is in the southernmost Croatian coast. The bay of Mali Ston continues onto the river mouth. This bay has been treated as a reserve for a long time because of its very rich and somewhat specific marine life (shells

Mljet National Park covers 31 km² and is the greenest corner of the European Mediterranean with spacious forests of holm oak, macchia and pine

etc.). Picturesque little islands surround Dubrovnik: Lokrum in the south, the Elafiti islands (Šipan, Lopud, Koločep and others) in the north. They all have lush evergreen vegetation; partly high macchia, partly pine woods. A rich cultural heritage, churches, monasteries, old summer houses, and nearby Dubrovnik, enhance the importance of these islands. As a reserve, Lokrum has been an inseparable part of Dubrovnik's identity for a long time, and the Elafiti, with the surrounding sea, are to be proclaimed a nature park.

A similar legal status is planned for the island of Lastovo, also one of the most forested Adriatic islands. Here, too, many smaller islands continue to the west and the east of the main island.

Finally, the lavish Mediterranean vegetation, combined with a complete botanical inventory, was one of the reasons for establishing a national park on the western third of the island of Mljet. Another reason, of equal value, was its specific shoreline with two lakes (the Big and Small Lake), in fact submerged karst depressions. They are interconnected and linked to the sea by almost invisible narrow channels, and give the impression of true lakes. Of course, the life in these »lakes« is specific and therefore of scientific interest.

The necklace of Croatian islands ends grandly with the »green« islands of Dubrovnik, and all of them form part of the magnificent littoral heritage that nature bestowed on Croatia.

Ivo Bralić

Chiton Olivatius spengler – chiton
Zonaria Pyruu – pear
Charonia Tritonis (L.) – triton

The historical nucleus of Split with Diocletian's Palace is inscribed in UNESCO's world cultural heritage list

Tomislav Marasović

CROATIAN ADRIATIC CITIES IN THE WORLD AND THE MEDITERRANEAN HERITAGE

In the cultural wealth that has for centuries accreted in the Croatian Adriatic region there are two categories of outstanding importance. These are made up of the historic cities that have found a place in two important international documents: the UNESCO list of the World Cultural Heritage and the Mediterranean list of One Hundred Historic Areas of Common Interest.

The UNESCO list is based on the International Convention of 1972, which set criteria for entry on the world heritage list. Any item entered on it must satisfy at least one of the Convention's criteria; it must:

- be a unique artistic or aesthetic achievement, a masterpiece of man's creativity;
- have had a notable influence on the development of architecture and art;
- be a unique or extremely rare antiquity;
- be the apex of its type in the field of culture, art or science;
- call to mind events or personalities of great historic importance.

Since 1979 two Croatian historic cities have been on that list: Split and Dubrovnik, and the Plitvice Lakes National Park.

Split's historic nucleus with Diocletian's Palace was acknowledged as part of the world cultural heritage according to almost all the above criteria.

It is the best-preserved example of any Roman palace. Archaeologists and art historians consider it a key structure both as a whole and in its individual parts. As a whole the Palace of the Emperor Diocletian in Split is a link between an extravagant imperial villa and a fortified camp with elements of a Hellenistic city. No other classical imperial residence, built before or after Diocletian's Palace, has so many original parts preserved. In themselves, these parts are exemplary monuments of their type. For example, the three facade walls and three land gates with double entrances are important examples of late-classical defence architecture. In the southern quarter of the Palace the substructure of the imperial apartments has been preserved, and contains about 50 vaulted halls. The Peristil is a unique open hall both in its role of an approach to the imperial apart-

Dubrovnik is the most beautiful jewel of Croatia's cultural heritage, a Gothic, Renaissance and baroque town included in UNESCO's world heritage list

ments and in architectural shape. Diocletian's Mausoleum-Temple is considered the prototype of many central late-classical and medieval structures. This, and many other parts of the Split Palace, have had a considerable influence on European architecture.

The medieval urban structure within and immediately to the west of Diocletian's Palace makes Split's historic nucleus especially valuable. There is a stratification of various periods and styles – pre-Romanesque, Romanesque, Gothic, Renaissance, baroque and others, and in many of them are masterpieces of older Croatian art.

Split's ancient nucleus is an important historic monument both in overall continuity and in each period in itself. Starting as the residence of the Emperor Diocletian, who was one of the most prominent rulers of the old world, it

witnessed important events in various chapters of Croatian history.

Unlike Split's historic stratification, the value of ancient Dubrovnik lies in the planned concept of a medieval city unique not only in the Adriatic region, but more widely. From the first early-medieval settlement on a rock, the city area gradually increased through planned construction that followed a town plan and concept. Even the great earthquake that destroyed much of Dubrovnik in 1667 did not mar the city's planned harmony because the new buildings were built according to the earlier town plan. All the citizens, from Rector to lowliest commoner, were conscious of urban harmony and this ensured Dubrovnik's present degree of preservation and its important role in the wider environs.

Panorama of Zadar. Zadar's historical nucleus is important because of many individual buildings, outstaning among which is St Donatus', the most monumental European pre-Romanesque 9th c. building.

Here, too, it is not only the harmony of the whole that is precious, but the sum of individual components. The town walls, fortified with towers and bastions, surround the city and are fine in themselves because of their specific western and eastern approaches, and because it is possible to walk around the whole city on them, enjoying an unrepeatable view of the internal structure and of the surroundings. As the city gradually developed, so did its main lines; the wide longitudinal street Placa (Stradun) between the West Gate and the Harbour was made by filling in an inlet. It separates the southern part of the city from the northern. Perpendicular to this longitudinal city axis stretches another – Luža – bordered by the historic buildings: the Rector's Palace, Town Hall, Cathedral, Church of St Blasius and Divona Palace.

Several other urban nuclei, like Trogir, Korčula and Ston, and individual buildings like the Church of St Donat in Zadar, the Amphitheatre in Pula and Euphrasius' Basilica in Poreč, are with much justification waiting to be entered in the list of the world heritage.

Mediterranean countries, signatories of the Barcelona Convention of 1975, established in the 1985 Geneva Declaration a special list of their most important historic cities under the name of One Hundred Historic Areas of Common Interest. The list includes six Croatian Adriatic cities: besides Dubrovnik and Split, these are Zadar, Trogir, Hvar and Korčula.

Zadar's historic nucleus, built on an elongated peninsula, grew out of the Roman colony Jader, a city of excep-

Panorama of Trogir. Trogir is called a town-museum because of a great number of monuments, the most important being St Laurence's Cathedral.

tionally regular residential blocks framed by a rectangular grid of streets. Medieval Zadar inherited a classical town plan, adapted to new conditions and surrounded by fortifications, which in the seventeenth century became a defence system. The importance of Zadar's historic nucleus is enhanced by notable individual buildings, outstanding among which is the pre-Romanesque rotunda of St Donat, an example of Carolingian architecture.

Classical urban tradition determined the basic shape of Trogir's historic nucleus, built on a round islet. The Greek-Roman nucleus has not been preserved (except remains here and there), but the medieval city as a whole is one of the most striking examples of its type in the eastern Adriatic. Here, too, there are individual buildings that

Panorama of Korčula. A town on an island of the same name, with St Mark's Cathedral, included by the Genoa Declaration from 1985 among the most important historic towns of the Mediterranean.

are considered »key monuments« of older Croatian art (the Cathedral with the Romanesque portal by Master Radovan and the Renaissance Chapel of St John), which add to the overall splendour.

Korčula, like Trogir, has almost completely preserved its ancient nucleus built on the crowded area of a natural peninsula. Korčula, however, did not develop as the transformation of a classical city. It was built in the Middle Ages according to a single plan.

Hvar is a another medieval city that developed without a classical foundation. Built on a rocky outcrop beside a well-protected harbour, it is an example of a planned city with a commoners' suburb that developed on the facing hill. The town square with its cathedral and public buildings links the two urban units into a single whole.

The town of Hvar on the island of Hvar. Included, with Split, Zadar, Trogir, Dubrovnik and Korčula, by the Barcelona Convention from 1975 and the Genoa Declaration from 1985, among »one hundred historic areas of common interest«.

ANIMA CROATORUM

I am tenderness, joy,
sorrow, scream and damnation.

I am the birth giver and the nursing mother.
I am your love: your maiden
and betrothed, wife and faithful one.
I am a warrior, martyr, captive
and sufferer: I count my steps on the edge
and fear that the thread might break
between to be and to dream. Between
to survive and to disappear, for I am
the reality and the dream of our sail which is dawning
and waiting for everything that has been sown
to fall onto the platter of the autumn
-feast: everything over which we watched and
everything that was possible and allowed...

I am that inclination. The invisible
foreboding, the flash of lightning and elevation.
Your recollection and song which the hand
records while they crucify me
leaving behind a red trail
of love and blood. I am the bread
which crumbles while you beckon
and wave good-bye to life. While
you grieve, rejoice. While you suffer,
doubt and while you are alone.

I am your No and your Yes.
Your How, Where and What.
Your proximity even when
you think that I am not there. Even then
I hover between you and the heights.
Between you and darkness. You and the depts.

I am your all: antiquity.
Your blood flow, which
pours into the River orf Endelssness.
I am your substance. I am
humanness, brotherhood and your
Croatianess: ark of your
kings and the nymph of your sea.

I am the indestructible part of you
woven of thread which binds:
ties and obliges. Your
strength and your charm. Your
peace and unrest. Sleep and wakefulness.
Constraint and crucifixion.

I am your land, your
rivers, your plains, you
sea and your mountains: roar, murmur,
boom and howl.

I am your Kaj, Ča and Što*
Your tongue, your body,
spirit, grave and tomb-stone.

I am the Only one
which is never forgotten:
covenant, testament, sign
and Amen.

Ivan Tolj
(Translated by: Vladimir Bubrin)

* What

83

The two old town
nuclei, Kaptol and
Grič, spread as on
the palm of a hand

View of Dolac Market and the north-west part of the town

A view of Kaptol, a medieval settlement which has many old houses. To the left stands the Franciscan Monastery and St Francis' church from the 13th c.

Lotrščak, one of the defence towers of Zagreb. It is the remains of the strong fortifications of 13th c. Gradec. Every day, exactly at noon, a cannon in fired from the tower to show the right time.

The Stone Gate, a Zagreb defence tower from 1266

Every ten minutes the funicular takes passengers from the Lower Town to Lotrščak and back

A view of Grič, one of the two old nuclei of Zagreb

Zagreb's most beautiful baroque building is St Catherine's church. It was renewed inside and out, and now hosts concerts. It is visited by tourists from many different countries. Special attention is attracted by the beautiful stucco decorations and a marble baroque altar by Francesco Robba from 1730.

St. Marks's church in Zagreb attracts tourists with mosaics of coats-of-arms on the roof and fine frescos

A view of Ban Jelačić Square. The square is just below Kaptol with the Cathedral and the seat of the Zagreb Bishopric, whose 900th anniversary is being celebrated in 1994.

Josip Jelačić was an important figure in Croatia's history. His statue on the square that carries his name, in the heart of Zagreb, was made by Anton Domenik korn in 1866.

Architect Viktor Kovačić designed the handsome building made of stone from the island of Brač in 1923, today the building of the National Bank of Croatia

Hrvatskih velikana Square

View of Preradovićev Square or the Flower Market, as people in Zagreb call it. It has the statue of the patriotic poet Petar Preradović by Ivan Rendić, from 1895. The Orthodox Church stands on the square.

Building of the Rectorate of Zagreb University, one of the oldest in Europe. Zagreb University was found on 23 September 1669.
Today it has 24 faculties, three art academies, four colleges and about ten scientific institutes.

The Well of Life by the sculptor Ivan Meštrović

Architect Viktor Kovačić designed St Blasius' church in Zagreb, introducing the modern spirit into Croatian architecture

The beautiful theatre square with a luxuriant and well tended park. The Croatian National Theatre is one of the most beautiful theatre buildings in Europe.

In front of the Mimara Museum stands a statue of the Croatian writer
Eugen Kumičić by Frano Kršinić

The Strossmayer Gallery is in the building of the Croatian Academy of Sciences and Arts, founded by Bishop Josip Juraj Strossmayer. It has a painting of *The Sacrifice of Abraham* by the Croatian painter Frederico Benković, which hangs next to Tintoretto, Bellini, Boticelli and other great artists of the world.

Air view of three parks: Zrinjevac, Strossmayerov Square and Tomislavov Square

Botanical Gardens

»The Lenuci Horseshoe«, Tomislavov Square with the statue of King Tomislav, a lovely park and the building of the Art Pavilion. The green parks that extend to the city centre make this the most beautiful part of Zagreb.

Statue of the first Croatian King Tomislav, who ruled Croatia from the Adriatic to the Drava, by R. Frangeš-Mihanović, 1931

Art Pavilion on Tomislavov Square. In the background is the building of the railway station

Fountain above the underground Importanne commercial and shopping centre. Esplanade Hotel in the background.

Shipbuilding Institute in Siget, New Zagreb.
It has 4 pools and 2 cavitation tunnels for
experimentally testing ships and ship propellers.

The new Croatian Television centre

Mirogoj, Zagreb's park graveyard with arcades and the church of Christ the King (architect Bollé, 1883), covers 72 hectares

Šalata sports park with a swimming pool, tennis courts, skating rink and other sports facilities

Architect Ferdo Wenzler designed Jarun. Three lakes, 700,000 m² of water area, facilities for 150,000 bathers and the most beautiful rowing course in Europe. The modern Mladost sports park near the banks of the Sava

The modern church of the Holy Cross in Siget in New Zagreb, designed by architects E. Seršić and M. Salaj

Zagreb's new mosque designed by Mirza Goleš and Džemal Čelić

In 1242 the Golden Bull of King Bela IV conferred on Zagreb the rights of free trade and holding fairs. The first international exhibition was held in Zagreb in 1864. The fair moved across the Sava in 1956 and now covers an area of 505,000 m², 180,000 m² of which is indoors.

Maksimir park-forest covers an area of 385 acres. It has 5 lakes and a Zoo, many pavilions, monuments and St George's church.

Medvedgrad, Memorial to the Defenders of Croatia, formerly a 13th c. royal and bishop's castle, nestling in the green of Zagrebačka gora mountain

The ruins of old Samobor castle, built in the 13th c., deserted in the 19th c. Samobor is an attractive town 20 km from Zagreb, a favourite Zagreb excursion place

Lužnica mansion, a baroque two-storey building west of Zaprešić

Laduč mansion, 19th c. Near Zaprešić

Classicist Januševac mansion near Zagreb, designed by the town architect of Zagreb, Bartol Felbinger

Novi Dvori near Zaprešić, the mansion of the Jelačić family

Baroque Bistra mansion, 17th c., with illusionist frescos in the hall

Krapina is the seat of the Krapina-Zagorje County, the legendary cradle of the Slavs Čeh, Leh and Meh. It has existed since 1193. Fossil remains of the Krapina neanderthal man were found in Hušnjakovo Cave and studied by D. Gorjanović-Kramberger (1899–1905).

Painted cincture in Trški vrh above Krapina. The church of St Mary of Jerusalem has fine frescos and a rich baroque interior (built by Josip Javornik, 1750).

Interior of the lovely church of St Mary of Jerusalem, Trški Vrh above Krapina

Vinagora, north-west of Pregrada. The charming vineyard landscape surrounds the baroque church of St Mary of the Visitation. Adam Ratkaj, Bishop of Senj, dedicated the church interior in 1713. In the nearby convent the Sisters of Charity care for elderly people. ▶

Old tower Krapina

Interior of sculptor Antun Augustinčić's gallery in Klanjec, his home town

St Martin's, a Gothic church reconstructed in the baroque style

Marija Bistrica, a famous medieval pilgrimage church

Krapinske toplice spa, besides many pools and hotels, there are also new convalescent buildings

Outdoor pools in Sutinske toplice

Tuheljske toplice spa with four outdoor and one indoor pool with running water, a hotel and convalescent centre

Stubičke toplice spa has radioactive water and the attractive and comfortable Matija Gubec Hotel

Varaždinske toplice spa dates from Roman times. Its medicinal waters cure many disorders. Today there are modern hotels and a convalescent centre here.

One of the seven interconnected lakes in Bedekovčina around the baroque mansions of the Bedeković family.

Veliki Tabor, a Renaissance castle with four towers and strong fortification walls. It got its final form in the 15th c. when the Renaissance towers and battlements were built.

Bela, an 18th c. mansion on the Ožegović estate

Veliki Tabor, detail

121

A view of the Peasant Revolt 1573 memorial area. The Peasant Revolt Memorial Museum is in the Oršić mansion. The monumental statue of Matija Gubec, leader of the revolt, is by the famous Croatian sculptor Antun Augustinčić.

Trakošćan Castle is the most visited of all the fifty or so castles and mansions in Croatian Zagorje. It used to belong to the Counts Drašković. A lake 2 km long, surrounded by thick woods, stretches beneath the castle.

Novi Marof, a fine baroque mansion with an evergreen park, today a convalescent centre

Belec, on the slopes of wooded Ivančica, is known for the votive church of St Mary of the Snow. Above the ornate baroque figures of angels and saints, the Pauline Ivan Ranger painted magnificent frescos on the walls and ceiling.

Miljana mansion, formerly owned by the Ratkaj family, has been completely restored by Franjo Kajfež, scientist and successful businessman. It has excellent late-baroque frescos of an astrological content.

St *Mary*
of the Snow

The Pauline order established a monastery in Lepoglava in 1400 and opened the first Croatian seconday school (1503) and high school, which became a university in the 17th c. The Gothic monastery chuch is one of the most important cultural monuments in Croatia. The main altar is the finest and fills the entire Gothic sanctuary.

Gothic St Mary's church in Lepoglava

Purga, baroque St George's chapel with frescos by Ivan Ranger, 1750

In Gorica, near Lepoglava, is the 17th c. baroque St John's chapel with frescos by Ivan Ranger (1731)

Klenovnik, a beautiful early-baroque 16th c. mansion with three rows of arcades and a chapel, today a hospital

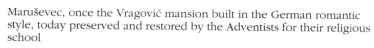

Maruševec, once the Vragović mansion built in the German romantic style, today preserved and restored by the Adventists for their religious school

Gothic church reconstructed in the baroque style in Varaždinske toplice

St Laurence's church in Lovrečan, built in the Gothic period

Interior of a village house in Kumrovec ethno village

Opeka Arboretum near Varaždin, detail from the park

Varaždin, once a strong army garrison by the river Drava, was the capital of Croatia for a long time. Today it is an industrial town, and an important centre of transit and excursion tourism. The town has a theatre built in 1861, a picture gallery, a museum in the old castle, a Jesuit and Franciscan church from the 17th c., a parish church and a Ursuline Convent.

Varaždin has many Renaissance and baroque mansions, the Patačić, Nitzky, Oršić and Keglević mansions and the County Hall

Medieval Varaždin developed in 1181, King Andrija II conferred the privileges of a royal free city on it in 1209, confirmed by King Bela IV in 1220. The most important monument is old Varaždin Castle, today completely restored. The Varaždin Baroque Evenings music festival has been held regularly since 1971.

Varaždin, main town square with the town hall built in 1523

Čakovec, the seat of Međimurje County, the economic, cultural and tourist centre of Međimurje

Old Čakovec castle was fortified in the 13th c. by the Čak lords. Today's castle was built in the 16th and 17th c. by the Croatian Counts Zrinski. Stari Dvor is today a museum and consists of two-storey buildings, and Novi Dvor is an enormous baroque mansion. After Zrinski's rebellion and execution in 1671 in Wiener Neustadt, the estate passed to Althan. The area around the castle developed into a market-town.

Exhibits from the museum

Kutina, a small town in the Moslavačka gora area, with a lovely baroque church

The rebuilt home for abandoned children that was completely destroyed by shelling.*

The new hotel in Lipik

Lipik spa known since Roman times, one of the best-known health resorts in Croatia. Although vandalized by the Serbian aggressors in 1991 and 1992, after its liberation Lipik is recovering and being rebuilt.

* It has the inscription in Croatian and English: Colonel Mark COOK, thank you for your great heart. These are words of thanks to the English colonel who financially helped the building of the home, together with many benefactors from the whole world (the German government and others).

Daruvar – Aquae Balissae, a town known for thermal springs since Roman times. A view of the park, sanatorium and sports-recreation centre.

Bjelovar, a town under Bilogora, 81 km from Zagreb. During the reign of Empress Maria Theresa it was an important military town with an orthogonal town plan and a large central square. There is a baroque church from 1772. This is the seat of the Bilogora-Moslavina County.

The Spoon, the symbol of Podravka factory, the greatest food (and soup) producer in Croatia

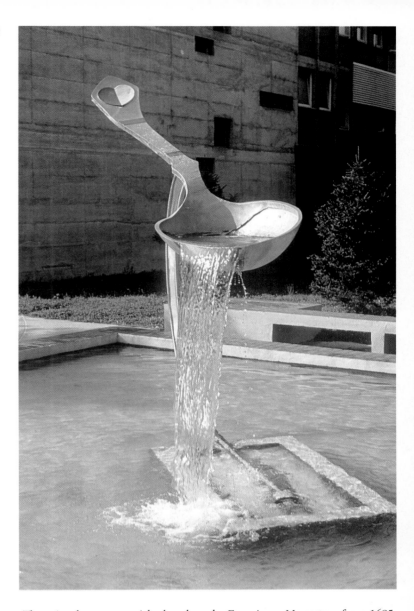

Koprivnica, since 1356 a free royal city in which the Croatian Sabor used to meet. There is a baroque parish church and a Franciscan Monastery from 1685.

139

Podravka is known worldwide as a producer of high-quality food with a varied and rich assortment of products

In front of the Podravka management building in Koprivnica stands another symbol of Podravka, *The Rooster*

A popular beer parlour in rustic style on the square in Koprivnica

Ivan Generalić, *Self Portrait*

Mato Generalić, *Village Musician*

Josip Generalić, *Grape Harvest*

Near Koprivnica is the village of Hlebine with the Primitive Art Gallery of Hlebine painters. The dominant figure was Ivan Generalić, one of the greatest primitive painters in the world. The Hlebine School is the world's most important group of primitive painters.

Mirko Virius, *Harvest*

Mirko Virius, *Coming Back from the Fields*

142

Ivan Generalić, *Cutting Wood*

Ivan Generalić, *The Stag Wedding*

143

Two paintings by Matija Skurjeni

Ivan Rabuzin, *My Homeland*

Ivan Lacković, *Winter*

Ivan Večenaj, *Boys Playing*

Mijo Kovačić, *On the River*

145

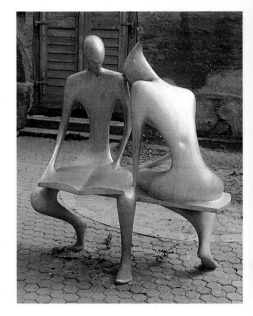

Križevci, bishopric church and residence of the
Greek-Catholic bishopric

Osijek, the seat of the Slavonija-Baranja County

Osijek, fortress

Vinkovci, centre

Vinkovci, Slavonian town on the river Bosut

Grape harvest in the Baranja vineyards

Ilok, a fortified town on the Danube

Slatina, mansion

Valpovo Castle, view from the north side of the Gothic chapel and tower

Watch-tower from the days of the Military March, today the Županja homeland museum

Valpovo Castle, view through the park

Virovitica, mansion of the Counts Pejačević

Atrium of the Franciscan Monastery in Slavonski Brod

The Eltz mansion in Vukovar, destroyed with the rest of the town in attacks on Croatia by Serbian aggressors

Našice, the Pejačević mansion from the 19th c.

The interior of Đakovo Cathedral, arranged by Josip Juraj Strossmayer, Bishop of Đakovo, great Croatian patron and founder of the Academy and the Strossmayer Gallery in Zagreb

Đakovo, with the monumental cathedral in the centre

Đakovo Embroidery, traditional folklore event

Đakovo Embroidery, girls on a horse cart

Scene from Ðakovo Embroidery, 1994

Mowing

Thoroughbred Lippizaner horses are bred in the stud-farm near Đakovo

Wheat fields in Slavonia

A field of poppies near Vinkovci

Slavonian forests near Koška village
Panorama of Slatina – a town between Virovitica and Valpovo

Nova Gradiška, St Theresa's church built in the late-baroque style, 1754–1756

Cernik mansion, a medieval castrum with late-baroque additions

Slavonski Brod, 18th c. fortress, zero class monument

Požega, the baroque Svetog Trojstva (Holy Trinity) Square

Wooden *kurija* of the Turopolje gentry

Wooden *kurija* in Lomnica near Velika Gorica

The most beautiful examples of wooden churches and local wooden architecture in Croatia are the chapels in Velika Mlaka and Lekenik. The picture shows the chapel of St Barbara in Velika Mlaka with a decorated vault and altar.

Topusko, a town on the river Glina under the forested Petrova gora mountain, known for radioactive waters since Roman times

Petrinja, an old military stronghold, has several churches and temporal buildings from the baroque and classicist periods

Baroque St. Magdalene's church in Sela

In Lekenik, near Sisak, the Lekenik SOS children's village was built, a Croatian village for orphans. Another village will be built in Ladimirovac. The world SOS Kinderdorf International organization is headquartered in Innsbruck, Austria.

The bridge over the Kupa in Sisak

Boats on the Kupa in Sisak

Sisak Castle. A strong fortress with a triangular ground-plan and three cylindrical towers on the corners. In the 1593 Battle of Sisak the Croats overwhelmed the Turks lead by Hasan-pasha Predojević.

Gothic church in Krašić reconstructed in the baroque style. Krašić was the birth place of Archbishop Stepinac, Croatian martyr, who spent his last days of confinement in the parsonage beside the church.

Pribić has the baroque St Mary's church, and Pribićki Strmec the Greek-Catholic bishop's palace. There is a neo-Byzantine church on an islet in the fish-pool.

The Mrežnica river

The Dobra river

Karlovac, a town on 4 rivers: the Kupa, Korana, Dobra and Mrežnica, 56 km from Zagreb. It was founded in 1579 by the Archduke Karlo (Charles) as a military stronghold against the Turks. The town has a theatre, a museum, lovely parks, beaches on the Korana, and the churches include the early-baroque church of the Holy Trinity.

Karlovac, a beach on the Korana

Ozalj, medieval castle above the Kupa

The first Croatian power-plant on the Kupa near Ozalj

In the 15th c. Dubovac Castle, shaped as an irregular rectangle, was built on a wooded hill above Karlovac

The Lokve reservoir in Gorski Kotar

Pastures in Gorski Kotar

Delnice is the main town in Gorski Kotar, situated on the Zagreb-Rijeka road. It is an important tourist centre, especially for mountain walking and winter sports.

Skrad mountain resort developed in the picturesque karst landscape of the forested hillside of Skradski vrh in Gorski Kotar

Risnjak in Gorski Kotar (1528 m)

Ski tracks on Bjelolasica in Gorski Kotar (1533 m)

Gorski Kotar is interesting for its valleys and rivers, for its limestone and dolomite caves, unexplored underground water courses, beautiful waterfalls

Lika offers a lot to interested tourists, primarily the Plitvice Lakes of European importance, part of the UNESCO World Heritage

On the spring of the river Gacka in Lika

Protected forests in Lika

On Velebit, the loveliest Croatian mountain

Velebit, an unlimited treasury for nature lovers, botanists, mountaineers and hill walkers

Poreč, a Roman town in Istria, one of the most beautiful monuments of Early-Christian art in the world. Between the 4th and the 6th c. were built the double oratorio, the basilica, the pre-Euphrasian Basilica, and the aisled apsidal Basilica of Euphrasius decorated with mosaics. Its pleasant climate, lovely beaches and modern holiday villages (Blue and Green Lagoon, islet of sv. Nikola etc.) have made Poreč the biggest tourist centre in Croatia.

Figure of a Bishop, Euphrasius with the Basilica, a beautiful mosaic of the finest art

Initials of Bishop Euphrasius, founder of the Basilica of Euphrasius

Atrium of the Basilica of Euphrasius in Poreč

Umag, inhabited since Roman times (Humagum), is an important tourist centre with plantation vineyards, a new marina and numerous sports facilities where the international Croatia Open tennis tournament is held every year

Vrsar, summer resort and fishing village on an Istrian peninsula

Novigrad, town and summer resort in west Istria, once the Roman settlement of Emona Neapolis. The town walls, a few late-Gothic houses and St Pelagia's 8th c. basilica have been preserved.

Dvigrad, a ruined town from the Romanesque-Gothic period

Višnjan, gothic church with 15th c. frescos

Motovun stands on the top of a conical hill in the romantic Mirna valley, surrounded by vineyards. It has well-preserved 13th to 15th c. walls, and a Renaissance loggia and church. Motovun's well-known red wines Teran, Refoško and Burgonj are highly appreciated and very popular.

Vrsar, St. Mary's church

Limski Kanal, a natural phenomenon of Istria with oyster beds

The graveyard chapel of St Mary on the Rocks

Pazin, a medieval town on a steep hill, 120 m above Jama, the swallow-hole down which the Pazinski potok disappears

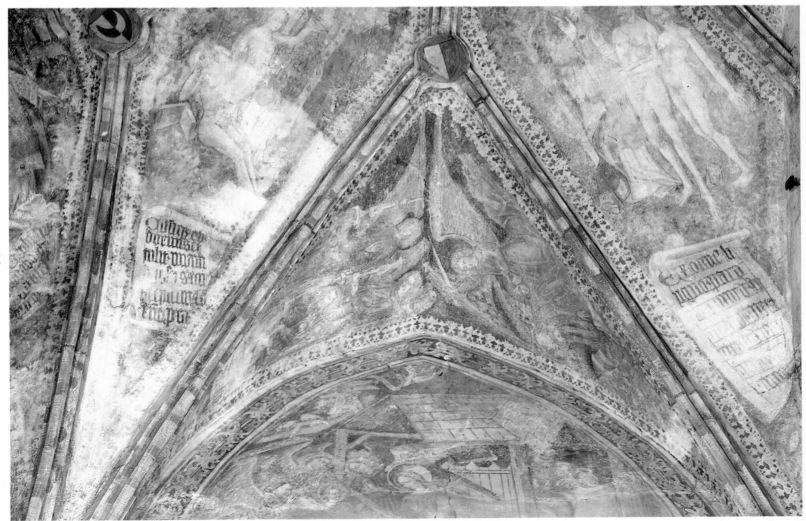

The parish church of St. Nicholas in Pazin is decorated with Gothic frescos

Baroque church in Žminj

The Gothic chapel of the Holy Trinity has frescos from 1471

Church of St Peter in the Wood, 13th c., with a Romanesque monastery and Renaissance cloister

Rovinj, indented coastline with Katarina and Crveni otok islands, a sea rich in fish, a national park, aquarium, protected beaches, hotels

Town gate in Rovinj   View of Rovinj   The monumental baroque church of St Euphemia

The Brijuni are the most interesting Istrian islands because of their classical excavations and beautiful landscapes. Fallow and roe deer live freely in woods and meadows that cover an area of 34 km².

A Roman temple from the Augustan period

Pula is the biggest Istrian town. A large Roman colony, then an arsenal and the largest Austrian war port, today an industrial (Uljanik Shipyard) and important tourist centre. The most important of the many Roman monuments is the Arena where opera performances and film festivals are held.

Pula, view of the port and town

A tourist town developed near Pula

Medulin, a well-known summer resort near Pula

Labin, a medieval town on a hill 320 m high, 5 km from the sea, with numerous cultural monuments from the 11th to the 17th c.

Mali Lošinj, a small town and harbour, a well-known summer and winter resort at the end of a long and narrow bay. Beautiful beaches, particulary on Čikat peninsula. In the last century the most important seafaring centre of the northern Adriatic.

Veli Lošinj is known for the houses of mariners who sailed all the world seas. Tourism is developing rapidly, and it is also known as a cure resort for respiratory disorders.

Rabac, summer resort with numerous hotels in lavish greenery

Mošćenička Draga, a popular summer resort

Lovran is one of the pearls under Mt Učka, with numerous cultural monuments, and a Romanesque and Gothic church with 15th c. frescos

Old Mošćenica

Volosko

Opatija, one of the most famous tourist resorts in the Mediterranean. It has beautiful parks, and numerous villas and hotels open to the public all through the year because Opatija is also a winter resort and a climatic health resort.

Admiral Hotel, A category, lies in a peaceful bay near the centre of the town

Old Trsat Castle, which offers a breathtaking view of Kvarner Gulf

Rijeka, a town that developed where the Riječina flows into Rijeka Bay, the third largest town in Croatia, the biggest Croatian port and shipbuilding centre
Rijeka, Koblerov Square

The Capuchin church in Rijeka

A small church surrounded with cypresses. There are hundreds of similar churches in the villages of the Kvarner and Croatia.

Rijeka's biggest church is St Vitus' Cathedral with a baroque dome

Scot bay

Bakar, a picturesque little town in Bakar Bay, trained generations of Croatian sailors in its nautical school

Novi Vinodolski, a picturesque town and well-known summer resort with a long tradition

Crikvenica, a well-known tourist resort in the Croatian Littoral

Karlobag – a town at the foot of Velebit, a developing tourist centre (the hotel village of the Industrogradnja firm)

Above Senj rises a very well-preserved fortress built in 1558. The Senj Missal was printed in the Senj Glagolitic printing press in 1494. The original is kept by the Franciscans on the island of Cres. The Croatian Academy of Sciences and Arts published a reprint in 1994 to mark its 500th anniversary.

Senj

The Rab cathedral's portal

Rab, the oldest part of the town lies on a peninsula. Its many bell-towers are one of the prominent features of this lovely and well-known tourist town.

The aisled cathedral, dedicated in 1177 by Pope Alexander III, is one of the oldest Romanesque buildings in Croatia

Haludovo Hotels in Malinska on the island of Krk, the highest-class hotels on the island and among the loveliest in the Croatian Adriatic

Vrbnik on the island of Krk. A town on a cliff above the sea, subject of a well-known folk song

Omišalj

215

Košljun, an islet on the island of Krk vith a 13–14th c. Franciscan Monastery. The great cultural wealth of Košljun monastery includes Glagolitic manuscripts and musical instruments.

The *Baška Tablet,* one of the oldest inscriptions
written in the Glagolitic alphabet

Krk on the island of Krk, Frankopan tower

Jurandvor, small Early-Christian church

217

Cres, folk costume

The of town Pag on the island of Pag

St. Mary a'church on the maine square in Pag

Nin, statue of Gregory of Nin. Behind the statue the pre-Romanesque church of the Holy Cross with the Prince Godežav inscription from the 11th c.

Nin, a peninsula rich in monuments from the oldest Croatian history

The beauty of the Romanesque St Anastasia's Cathedral dominates Zadar, the most important historic town of north Dalmatia and the seat of the Zadar-Knin County

Pre-Romanesque St Nicholas' church near Nin

Romanesque Benedictine church of St Chrysogonous, 11th–12th c.

Early-Christian basilica of St Simon

Benedictine church of St Mary with a Romanesque bell tower from 1105

Bust of a saint from the collection *The Gold and Silver of Zadar*

Tablet with a miniature crucifiction, end 13th c., from the collection *The Gold and Silver of Zadar*

Vittore Carpaccio, *St Anastasia*

Vittore Carpaccio, *St Martin,* end 15th c.

The Arrival of King Ludovik of Anjou in Zadar, scene from the Chest of St Simon by the goldsmith Frances of Milan, 1377–1380

Polyptych from Ugljan

229

The Square of Five Wells

Roman column in Zadar

Town gate in Zadar

Atrium of the Franciscan Monastery with Renaissance cloister, 16th c. Beside it stands St Francis' church, 13th c.

231

Vrgorac, the tower in which the great Croatian poet Tin Ujević was born

Alka contestants in Sinj. In the *Sinjska alka* tournament riders in old warrior dress compete in hitting a hanging ring at full gallop, celebrating the historic victory over the Turks.

Fortified Vrlika between Mts Dinara and Svilaja

Knin, an old Croatian Town. View of the Fortress

Petar Šimundža, *Alka* champion for 1994

The Old tower in Drniš above the river Čikola

Otavice, the village of the Meštrović family in which the great Croatian sculptor built the family mausoleum. In nearby Drniš the memorial collection has several of Meštrović's works.

Iž, between Pašman and Ugljan, in lush Mediterranean vegetation. Mali Iž has an Early-Croatian church from the 11th c. and Veli Iž a 14th c. parish church.

The island of Ugljan has many medieval churches in the villages of Preko, Kali, Ugljan and Sutimišćica

Dugi otok has magnificent beaches (Telašćica, Soliščica, Pantera, Sakarun) and historic remains: from Illyrian excavations and Roman *villae rusticae*, to pre-Romanesque churches

Sali, the main village on Dugi otok, was named after its salt flats. Several hundred fishing boats from Sali catch about 800 tons of fish every year.

Biograd na moru is surrounded by rich pine woods and lovely beaches. It also has a new marina. It was first mentioned in the 10th c., and in the 11th c. it was a bishopric and the capital of the King of Croatia.

Pakoštane, a summer resort of the international French Club Méditerrané

237

Lake Vrana is rich in fish. This large fresh-water lake is 14 km long and 2 km wide

Murter, a delightful tourist resort near the most beautiful Croatian archipelago, the Kornati Islands. It is a tourist, shipbuilding and fishing village. Slanica is the most beautiful beach on Murter.

View of the Kornati Islands

Women of Zlarin in their beautiful and elegant costumes adorned with corals. Processing corals is a tradition in Zlarin

Tijesno, a pretty tourist village near Vodice

Vodice is a charming and attractive tourist resort with hotels, lovely beaches and a new marina

The Festival of the Child has been held for years in Šibenik as a traditional international children's event

Šibenik choir on the cathedral square

Renaissance town loggia, 16th c.

Šibenik, St Jacob's Cathedral, 15th c. This masterpiece of Croatian architecture was begun by Juraj Dalmatinac, and completed by Nikola Firentinac.

243

The apses of Šibenik Cathedral have a row of 74 sculptures showing human heads, rendered with sharp realism. They were made by the cathedral's architect Juraj Dalmatinac.

The dome, aisles and Renaissance vault built of stone slabs, are a unique feature in the history of architecture. This was achieved by Nikola Firentinac when he completed the Šibenik Cathedral.

Šibenik was founded at the time of Croatian kings and was mentioned for the first time in the deed of gift of Croatian King Petar Krešimir IV in 1066. The oldest part of the town developed under the Fortress of St Anne, and Šubićevac Fortress is also partly preserved.

Skradin, formerly the important Roman town of Scardona. Beyond Skradin the Krka is navigable and widens into Lake Prokljan.

The architect Sammicheli (1540–1547) built the Fort of St Nicholas with a monumental Renaissance gate at the harbour entrance

Primošten is a village on an islet connected to the mainland by an embankment. Its inhabitants make their living from tourism, fishing and wine production (the well-known Babić wine)

A view of Trogir from the sea. In the foreground stands Fort Kamerlengo

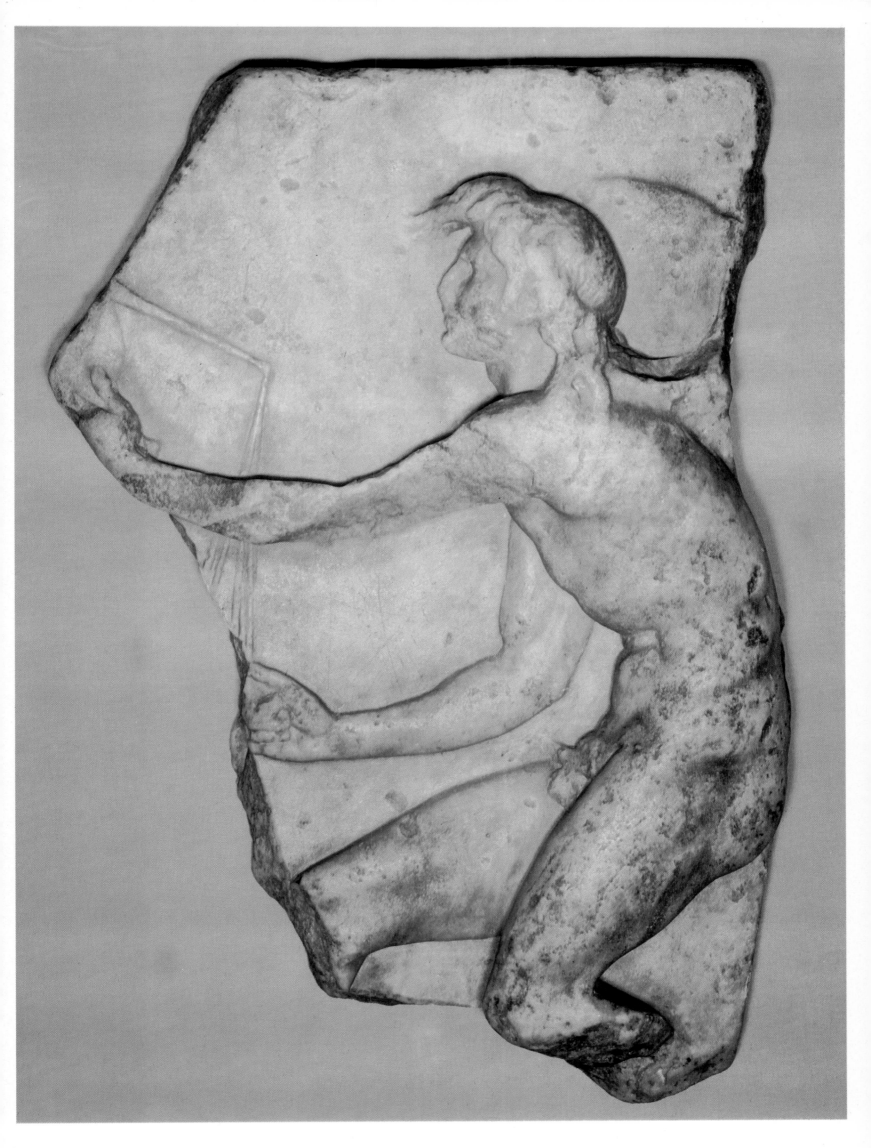

Kairos, the god of opportunity, from the 1st c., in the Benedictine Convent in Trogir

Chapel of Ivan the Blessed in Trogir Cathedral, by Nikola Firentinac, the first Renaissance work in Croatia. It has harmonious Renaissance proportions and expressive sculptures by Nikola Firentinac, Ivan Duknović and Andrija Aleši.

The bell tower of St Laurence's Cathedral was built in a mixture of styles: Romanesque, Gothic and Renaissance

Blaž Jurjev, *Our Lady in the Rose Garden,* a masterpiece by the Croatian Gothic painter. Blaž Jurjev of Trogir painted between 1412 and 1450 and left a strong mark on the history of Croatian and world art.

Trogir marina

There are nine charming villages between Solin and Trogir, including the seven Kaštels: Kaštel Sućurac, Kaštel Gomilica, Kaštel Kambelovac, Kaštel Lukšić, Kaštel Stari, Kaštel Novi and Kaštel Štafilić. The picture shows Kaštel Gomilica.

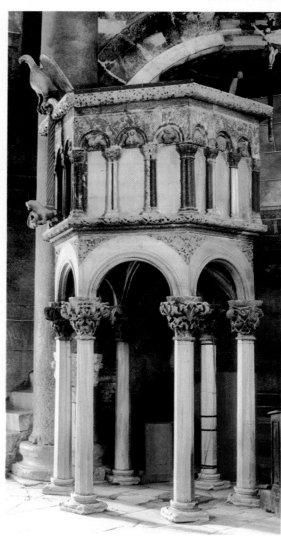

254

Romanesque bell tower of St Doimus' Cathedral, 13th–16th c.

SICUT CER
VUS DESI
DERAT AD FON
TES AQVARUM

ITA
DESI
DERAT

ANIMA
MEAADTE
DEVS

Figural mosaic with
verses from the 42nd
Psalm, David's
Salona, early 5th c.

Ruins of Salona, one
of the greatest
Roman excavation
sites in this part of
Europe

The city of Split developed from Diocletian's Palace. This 3rd c. palace is the best-preserved Roman palace in the world. Detail from the peristyle.

Radun, St George's, Early-Croatian church

St Jerome's church on Mt Marjan

Medieval hermit's cave on Mt Marjan

Old town hall on Narodni Square

Croatian National Theatre in Split

Statue of Marko Marulić, the great Croatian poet, by Ivan Meštrović, on Braće Radića Square

Museum of Croatian Archaeology

Ivan Meštrović Gallery in Split

Ivan Meštrović, statue of Gregory of Nin, a great fighter for Glagolitic liturgy, in front of the Golden Gate

View of Split sports' centre, the marina and the city of Split

Klis on a hill 360 m high near Split, in the 11th c. the court of Croatian rulers

Omiš, a small town nestling under the great canyon at the mouth of the Cetina. Statue of Mila Gojsalić (by Ivan Meštrović), who sacrificed her life for the freedom of the Poljice Republic in fights against the Turks.

Brela, summer resort at the beginning of the Makarska Riviera. The thick pine woods stretch to the shingle beaches and the crystal clear sea.

Makarska, a town, harbour and the tourist centre of the Makarska Riviera. Here, under the stark cliffs of Biokovo, are some of the most beautiful shingle beaches of the Adriatic. The town has the 14th c. Franciscan Monastery with a fine collection of shells and the Mountain and Sea Institute founded by the Franciscan Jure Radić, scientist and humanist, with his associate Brother Frano Car and the tireless Sister Edit, who continued his work after his death.

Ložišća with interesting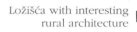
rural architecture

Šolta, a picturesque and woody island facing Split

Supetar, the main town on the island of Brač with a long sandy beach and hotels

Sutivan, a bathing resort with the mansion of the poet J. Kavanjin

The island of Brač is the third largest Adriatic island (395 km²). Its highest peak is Vidova gora (778 m). It has rich pine woods near the sea and the interior is under vineyards and olive groves. Diocletian's Palace in Split was built of Brač stone, and Postira, Pučišća, Selca and Splitska have stone quarries.

Bobovišća, statue of the Croatian poet Vladimir Nazor

Povlja, Early-Christian font, 5th c.

Milna, a summer resort on the west side of the island

Postira, sandy and shingle beaches, hotels, a camp and a 15th c. parish church

Bol on the island of Brač. Its shingle promontory shifts according to the direction of the wind and waves.

Pučišća with the Romanesque-Gothic St George's church

269

Hvar, an island with a crystalline cobalt-coloured sea, vineyards, olive groves, aromatic herbs

A view of the harbour and Fort

The 16th c. Renaissance cathedral
on a lovely Renaissance square has
a rich treasury

Vrboska on Hvar, Renaissance fortified church

Starigrad on Hvar, Renaissance mansion of the poet Petar Hektorović, 15th c.

Jelsa on the island of Hvar with the baroque St John's church on the square

Vis, a small town on the island of the same name, founded (Issa) by the old Greeks in the beginning of the 4th c. B.C. Komiža on the island of Vis. Large shingle and sandy beaches in lush vegetation. The castle in the harbour and the Renaissance church are from the 16th c.

St. Mark's Cathedral in Korčula

Moreška, an old sword dance

Korčula on the island of Korčula

Vela Luka on the island of Korčula

275

Orebić on the island of Pelješac

Vineyards on Pelješac, where the well-known wines Grk and Dingač are made

New hotel in Trpanj on Pelješac peninsula

Ston, a fortified town on Pelješac peninsula with salt flats, and oyster beds. Above Ston stands the pre-Romanesque St. Michael's church with frescos and a painted crucifixion by Blaž Jurjev.

Metković in the picturesque valley of the Neretva with fruit and vegetable plantations

Minčeta Tower in Dubrovnik at the beginning of the south town walls, a masterpiece of Croatian fortificational architecture.
It was begun by M. Michelozzi and completed by Juraj Dalmatinac.

East gate of Ploći

Dubrovnik walls, a symphony of fortificational architecture.

Panorama of Dubrovnik, the most beautiful town on the Croatian Adriatic

St. Blaise, protector of Dubrovnik

Dubrovnik, Renaissance, church of the St Saviour. Beside it stands Onofrio's Large Fountain, the final point of the town waterworks built in the 15th c.

Dubrovnik Cathedral from the 18th c. Architect A. Buffalini of Urbin.

Nikola Božidarević, triptych *Virgin and Child,* 1517, in St Mary's church

The Virgin with SS Blasius and Francis in the Dominican Museum is by the Neapolitan painter Antonio de Belisso, mid-17th c.

St Blaise's church. The new baroque church was designed by Marino Gropelli in 1706-1714. In front of it is the symbol of a merchant city, Orlando's Column, with a 14th c. flagpole. Great celebrations are organized in Dubrovnik every year on the feast of St Blaise.

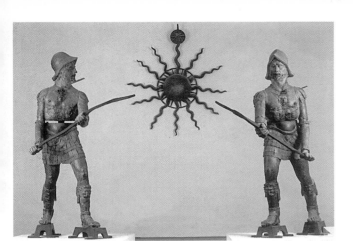

Sponza Palace and town belltower. The belltower has a two-tone bell cast by Ivan Krstitelj-Rabljanin in 1506. Two bronze jacks, the Zelenci, strike the hours.

The Rector's Palace was built by Onofrio di Giordano della Cava in the Gothic-Renaissance style.

Cavtat, a town on the edge of Župa bay with subtropical vegetation, fine beaches, and bays with luxurious hotels and camps. The Croatia hotel complex is built on a rock over the sea. Cavtat was an old Illyrian settlement, Roman Epidaurum destroyed by the Avars in the 6th c., and after 1302 it was a part of the Dubrovnik Republic. The Renaissance cloister in the Franciscan Monastery, the baroque parish church and the mausoleum of the Račić family, by Ivan Meštrović.

Tourist resort on the island of Mljet

Lastovo, forested island in south Dalmatia

The Elafiti islands lie between Pelješac peninsula and Dubrovnik

PASTORAL CARE FOR CROATS ABROAD

Croatian Catholic emigrants – the concern of the Overall Church. For over a hundred years the Catholic Church has systematically kept in touch with its emigrants, providing for their pastoral guidance through laws and regulations. All Church activities in the field of migration are based on three major documents: the Apostolic Constitution *Exsul Familia* of 1952, the Instruction *De pastorali migratorum cura* of 1969 and the *Codex Iuris Canonici* of 1983. Care basically consists of sending priests of their own people and language to larger groups of emigrant Catholics, to organize and head ethnic parishes, missions and curacies in accord with the regulations of the local Church. Today several thousand of such ethnic centres for spiritual guidance exist, primarily attracting immigrants of the first and second generation, and all others who wish to receive the Gospel message in their mother tongue and express their faith in the content and on the foundations of their cultural heritage.

For a whole century emigrant Croatian Catholics have enjoyed organized ethnic spiritual guidance, which is part of the overall concern of the Church and corresponds to that enjoyed by Catholics of other nationalities. It all began in August 1894 when Dobroslav Božić, a priest from Đakovo sent to the United States of America by Bishop Strossmayer, celebrated a mass for all Croatian Catholics at mass in Pittsburgh. As a result the parish of St Nicholas was founded, and it celebrated its centenary on 14 August 1994.

Croatian parishes and missions the world over. There are four groups of Croatian emigrants: Croats in neighbouring countries; Croats in overseas countries; Croatian workers in West Europe; the newest refugees – victims of greater-Serbian aggression against Croatia, Bosnia and Hercegovina in 1991 and after. The religious needs of Croats in neighbouring countries, who were separated from their mother country after the disintegration of Austria-Hungary, are met by the local Church that has organized their parishes over several centuries. Today there are over seventy such parishes (in Austrian Burgenland, Hungary, Romania), and they are under the exclusive jurisdiction of their local bishops. The disintegration of Yugoslavia left a large number of Croatian Catholics outside Croatia, Bosnia and Hercegovina (in Slovenia, Serbia, Montenegro). They will be called Croats

Msgr. Stanković presents with the cardinals Šeper and Kuharić to Pope John Paul II the anthology "The Catholic Church and The Croats Living Abroad", 1980

Congress on spiritual guidance and the emigrants, Vatican

in neighbouring countries, they too have their parishes with priests and bishops and are closely connected with the Church in Croatia. The Council for Croatian Migration of the Croatian Bishops' Conference, today headed by Archbishop Marijan Oblak of Zadar, has organized Pastoral Guidance for Croats Abroad for all other groups of Croatian Catholics outside Croatia. Since 1969, Msgr. Vladimir Stanković, priest of the Zagreb Archdiocese, has been national director of the Committee for Pastoral Guidance for Emigrants. He supervises the work of two bureaus, one in Rome, the other in Zagreb, that coordinate the work of 197 Croatian ethnic parishes and missions in overseas countries and in countries of Western Europe. There are 118 such missions in West-European countries: 86 in Germany, 8 in Austria, 8 in Switzerland, 4 in France, 3 in Sweden, 2 in Belgium, 2 in Italy and one each in Great Britain, the Netherlands, Norway, Denmark and Luxembourg. The USA has 39 Croatian parishes, Canada 19, Australia 14, South America 4 (Argentina, Peru, Venezuela), New Zealand 2, and South Africa one – overseas countries have a total of 79 Croatian parishes and missions. The largest number of Croatian parishes and missions were founded in the last 25 years, a total of 104. In the same period 180 priests were sent abroad from Croatia, Bosnia and Hercegovina for pastoral care, by decree of the Croatian Bishops' Conference. Today the Croatian foreign pastorale includes 252 priests, 150 in countries of West Europe and 102 in overseas countries. Besides priests, 263 nuns, lay catechists and social workers also work among Croatian Catholics abroad, making a total of 515 persons. In overseas countries Croatian Catholics in most cases have their own churches, parish halls and other buildings that they built themselves. In countries of Western Europe the local Church

has placed parish churches and chapels at their disposal, but everywhere they have their own parish halls, and often also premises for religious instruction and meetings, and offices for church social workers. Croatian bishops and the heads of religious orders choose priests to serve abroad and recommend them to the Croatian Bishops' Conference. Today two thirds of the priests in the foreign pastorale are religious priests and one third are diocesan, and they come from all the religious orders and bishoprics. Most are Franciscans, primarily from the Split and Mostar, and then from the Zagreb, Sarajevo and Zadar Province. In the USA a growing number of priests are the children of Croatian immigrants. Priests in all other countries were born and educated in Croatia. Unlike the priests of other emigrant groups, Croatian priests are relatively young because their numbers are regularly renewed by new arrivals from Croatia. This is also true of nuns and social workers. The independence of Croatian pastoral care abroad and the greater or lesser use of the Croatian language depends on the degree of integration and assimilation into the new environment, and on the arrival of new immigrants. In 1994 many ethnic parishes in the USA were closed down – including some Croatian parishes founded at the beginning of the twentieth century. At the same time there is a rapid influx of new believers into some West-European countries, which has resulted in increased activities of Croatian missions.

Main foreign pastoral activities. The main activity of every foreign pastorale, the Croatian included, is to spread the Gospel. This includes varied pastoral activities of the kind carried out in all Catholic parishes, from basic pastoral work to special undertakings. The most conspicuous form of parish and mission life is mass, usually attended by believers who come from great distances. Although regular services in Croatian are held in over five hundred places in Western Europe, many settlements where Croats live are not near such churches and people must travel a long way to reach them. They come with pleasure, not only to hear mass but to meet their compatriots and for other reasons, and Sunday mass is usually the main meeting-place for people from varied parts of Croatia and of varied political outlooks. Receiving the sacraments at mass: baptism, confession, communion, matrimony and confirmation, are all part of their Church life. Bishops from Croatia almost always go to countries of Western Europe, and often to overseas countries as well, for confirmation, making it a great parish and family festivity. The catechism in Croatian is considered very important for young people to perfect their mother tongue, but in places where emigration is of longer standing religious instruction is carried out in the language of the home country because young people would not understand it in the language of their fathers and mothers, which they can hardly speak. Priests pay great attention to disseminating religious publications from Croatia. In some countries they publish real periodicals, while every parish or mission has its weekly bulletin. In some countries Croatian radio hours are well organized, completely conducted by priests or with a section concerning religious life, and television programmes are being started, too. Priests make efforts to procure for their parishioners as many Croatian religious books as they can, especially the Bible, and also novels or books of a historic or cultural content. In overseas countries Croatian parishes have Saturday schools for religious instruction, teaching the Croatian language, history, geography, Croatian songs and folk dances. In countries of Western Europe priests have contributed greatly to the foundation of supplementary Croatian schools in which they hold religious instruction themselves. Croatian folklore is cultivated with great care in the parishes and missions, and many folk-dancing groups, festivals and performances are organized on a regional and national level. Pilgrimages in which a great number of people take part are especially popular. Matches and games are organized for young people in various sports, most of all in soccer. In Germany the Bible Catechist Olympiad has been very popular for many years as part of the Croatian Catholic Youth Gatherings, and in recent years it has joined similar knowledge quizzes in religious truths and Croatian church history held in Croatia. The prayerbook-songbook *Glory to God* and the cantual of the same name, published by the Central Croatian Pastoral Office in Frankfurt, is an especially strong link between emigrants and the Church in Croatia. Almost one hundred thousand copies have been distributed free of charge to all the parishes and religious congregations in Croatia. Many parishes and missions have lending libraries with a large number of books from which emigrants borrow books expanding their cultural horizons. On certain occasions priests donate books about Croatia in their own language to local bishops, their associates and public figures, and also to members of their own parishes who can no longer speak Croatian. All these and other activities were and remain an integral part of foreign pastoral work, and they were especially important in the time of the Yugo-communist regime which had a negative attitude to Croatian emigrants, and especially to Croatian missions and parishes, primarily because they always nurtured the idea and desire for a free Croatia. Today there are great

Cardinal Kuharić confirming Croatian children in Göppingen

Mother Theresa with Croats in Oslo, Norway

In the new Croatian church in Hobart, Tasmania, 1993
With Croatian priests in Los Angeles, 1991

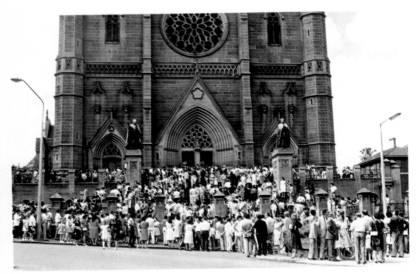

Croats in front of the Cathedral in Sydney, 1983

Croatian church in Ottawa, Canada

Croatian St Jerome's church in the Republic of South Africa, 1993

prospects for various Croatian societies and associations abroad, and for official representatives of the Republic of Croatia, to take over some of these mission activities. However, believers still mostly gather around our mission and parish centres in which they place the greatest reliance and which will continue to remain the most important and most popular centres not only of religious, but also of the national and cultural identity of Croatian emigrants. At the time of the Yugo-communist regime various Yugoslav clubs

and consular and diplomatic offices were the greatest opponents of Croatian foreign pastoral centres, hindering their work. Today, on the contrary, the personnel of Croatian embassies and consulates support them and even themselves participate in various parish activities. Missions also cooperate with the Croatian Foundation Homeland, the Croatian World Congress and with various cultural societies, political parties and fraternal associations like the Croatian Catholic Union and the Croatian Fraternal Union. But even as parishes and missions, through their diverse activities, affirm everything Croatian and always work for good relations between the host country and the Republic of Croatia, they take care not to descend into the arena of everyday political life and do not identify themselves with any political party, either in Croatia or among emigrants.

In all countries the Catholic Church has organized a special social service for emigrants and guest workers. The first to offer various social services were priests and they often still do so, helping people in their most varied needs. After that special social wellfare work was organized in some countries on the national and bishopric level within the framework of Caritas. In that sense most was done in Germany, which has a branching network of Caritas social offices for foreign workers, including Croats. About one hundred highly-qualified Croatian social workers actively cooperate with priests to the good of both Croats and Muslims and all others who turn to them in need, and they are making especially great efforts to help newly-arrived families of refugees. Although social offices and the social workers who work in them are not institutionally part of the pastoral mission, they are nevertheless strictly a church structure that is closely connected with the local bishop, under whose guidance they work.

Help to Croatia, Bosnia and Hercegovina in the Homeland War. At the very beginning of greater-Serbian aggression against Croatia in 1991, Croatian Catholic missions and parishes were the first to begin helping the Homeland. Before any foreign Caritas or other humanitarian association, Croatian priests began sending food, clothes, footwear, medicines and sanitary material, and also many ambulances. They responded to Cardinal Kuharić's appeal and collected money from their parishioners which they sent to the Croatian Caritas, diocesan Caritases and caritative activities of their religious congregations. Countless lorries and containers were sent to Croatia, Bosnia and Hercegovina by Croatian parishes and missions abroad. Although with diminished intensity, those activities are still continuing in the most varied forms: helping the Bureau for Refugees and Displaced Persons, hospitals, medical centres, the wounded, invalids, war orphans, schools and various regional clubs, destroyed or damaged churches, chapels, parsonages and monasteries. Croatian pastoral workers encouraged their parishioners to donate to the national fund for Croatia and for all worthy activities to the benefit of the Homeland and its postwar renewal. They are a permanent Croatian lobby that spreads the truth about Croatia, Bosnia and Hercegovina, not only in church circles, but especially offering the media exact information about what is happening in this region. Priests, social workers and pastoral associates are especially to be praised for the fact that local Caritas organizations and other humanitarian institutions sent their convoys with food and medication to Croatia, Bosnia and Hercegovina. Workers in the foreign pastoral care did great work on the reception and care for tens of thousands of new refugees who came to their countries. Wherever those banished Croats and Muslims came, everywhere they encountered an organized network of pastoral and social aid making it easier for them to find their bearings and adapt to new conditions. There is no doubt that every Croatian foreign mission and parish could publish a book with data about help rendered in the Homeland War.

Perspectives and future of the foreign pastoral care. As part of the Catholic Church and overall world migrations, Croatian emigrants and their foreign pastorate will in future pass through similar phases as other ethnic groups. Migration will persist, people will continue to go into the world, but we hope that when peace comes more Croats will be coming to Croatia than leaving it. Still, we must count on the fact that a great majority will not return. They must be the special concern of both the Croatian state and the Croatian Church. Thus Croatian missions will continue to play an important role in the life of Croatian emigrants, but that role and the specific work it entails will adapt to new conditions. While we are beginning to see the slow but systematic closing down of traditional Croatian parishes in the USA, while even in West Europe our young people know less and less Croatian, while tendencies in the local Church are becoming increasingly restrictive almost everywhere, mostly due to a lack of clergy, and attempts are increasingly being made to integrate foreign missions into the regular pastoral work of the local Church, the new wave of refugees in some countries is suddenly rejuvenating the emigrant community and giving Croatian missions a new and more dynamic life. Interest in Croatian folklore is growing among young people, they like visiting Croatia, prefer Croatian mass to that in the nearby local church, fill halls in which Croatian performances are taking place, and many fought in the Homeland War. Both State and Church must seek and quickly find new approaches to those young people to prevent them from being lost either as Croats or as Catholics. Although everything must be done to give them a chance to learn Croatian, in the countries of West Europe they should receive religious instruction in the language of the country they live in to enable better understanding of what is being taught, and at the same time they should learn the basic religious truths, prayers and hymns in Croatian, as is already the case in overseas countries. The state will have to publish more books about Croatia in foreign languages so that new generations of Croatian emigrants may get to know and love the land of their ancestors. As part of the Catholic Church, Croatian foreign missions and parishes will educate their faithful for easy and successful integration into the life of the local Church when they leave the Croatian ethnic environment. Thus missions will become a bridge between the two shores, the Croatian and local Church, a role imposed on them by the very character of migration, by common sense, and also by the guidelines and regulations of the Catholic Church. As we enter the second century of organized pastoral care for Croatian Catholics abroad, our parishes and missions will seek for new paths on the basis of a century of experience and respond to new challenges in the spirit of the words of Pope Paul VI: »Pastoral care for migrants always attracted the maternal care of the Church, which truly, through the centuries, never stopped helping in various ways those who were forced to go far from their homeland, like the banished Christ to Egypt with the family of Nazareth« (Motuproprio »Pastoralis migratorum«).

Msg. Vladimir Stanković

Croatian folklore festival, 12 February 1994, Ludwigshafen, Germany

Cardinal Kuharić leading the Way of the Cross in Eisiedeln, Switzerland

Archbishop Franić with nuns in Puente Piedra, Peru, 1971

Present of the Croatian parish in Toronto to the Croatian Caritas

Pope John Paul II with Msgr. Vinko Puljić, Archbishop of Sarajevo, in Zagreb, September 10 1994

Croatian mothers from Vukovar with the Holy Father in Zagreb, September 11 1994

IN THE VATICAN THE POPE SPOKE
TO PILGRIMS ABOUT HIS TRIP
TO CROATIA

Dear brothers and sisters, as you know, last Saturday and Sunday I had the joy of going to Croatia and visiting the Zagreb Church to mark the 900th anniversary of the foundation of the Zagreb Archbishopric. The original intention had been for this visit to be part of a wider pastoral pilgrimage that was also to include Belgrade and Sarajevo.

I thank the Lord for allowing me to bring support and encouragement to everyone striving for peace in the Balkans. I also want to express once more my gratitude to those who invited me to that beloved country, especially to Mr Franjo Tuđman, President of the Republic of Croatia, and to Cardinal Franjo Kuharić, Archbishop of Zagreb. I also thank all who worked to achieve the success of the visit and the very numerous believers who, at the cost of great sacrifice, desired to gather around Peter's successor.

The Croatian people were the first Slavs to encounter Christianity. Their conversion, which began in the seventh century, was the work of missionaries from Rome, and was also under the beneficial influence of the holy brothers SS Cyril and Methodius, Apostles of the Slavs. The Croatian nation established a bond of singular unity with the Holy Seat very early, which during the centuries has gradually developed and deepened. Pope John X addressed the first Croatian King Tomislav (910–930) calling his subjects »the most special sons of the Holy Roman Church« (*specialissimi filii Sanctae Romanae Ecclesia*). In the period of the Otoman invasion of Europe, Leo X conferred on the Croats the title: »The strongest shield and bulwark of Christianity« (*Scutum saldissimum et antemurale christianitatis*). This title had a great and real meaning in the history of faith and in the sanctity achieved by the Croatian people, and is also finely expressed in the nine centuries of life of the Zagreb Church.

In our century Croatia was gripped by the drama that took place in the Balkans in the years between the two world wars, and after the Second World War in events involving the Yugoslav federation and its later crisis.

An outstanding figure of the Croatian Church in those decades of suffering was Cardinal Alojzije Stepinac, Archbishop of Zagreb, who with fearless courage testified to faith in the Gospel and loyalty to the Apostolic See. But he was not alone. With him were numerous shepherds, right until the present, who shared the suffering of the Croatian people sustaining the torch of faith and hope in the faithful.

Today the Church continues to work with those same intentions, and in Croatia it is sincerely cooperating with other Christian and non-Christian communities and all people of good will.

Beloved, a visit long anticipated has been realized. It was preceded by an intense period of prayer marked by many endeavours, among which we must mention the »million rosaries« for the success of the visit.

The trip climaxed in the celebration of holy mass. In this joined an infinitive multitude of believers who with great fervour prayed, sang and invoked the Lord's blessing to enable them to face the hardship of the present and build a better future.

The enthusiasm of the young gave me comfort and hope. In it I saw the readiness of new generations to accept and realize in their own lives the message of reconciliation I brought them in the name of Christ. I cannot here not mention the meeting with refugees and pilgrims from one hundred and fifty destroyed parishes in Croatia, and with those who came from Bosnia and Hercegovina to whom I again confirmed my resolution to visit Sarajevo as soon as circumstances permit.

To bring peace to these tormented countries it is important to continue to pray to God persistently and with conviction. But if such great good a new period of mutual understanding and progress is to be achieved it is also necessary, as I resolutely declared in Zagreb, to forgive and seek forgiveness. The duty of forgiveness stems from our common position of sons of the Heavenly Father, who excludes no one from the tenderness of His love, regardless of race, culture and nationality.

Thus I call on you all to join me in prayer to God for the beloved Church of Zagreb, for the inhabitants of Croatia, and especially for the inhabitants of Sarajevo and Bosnia and Hercegovina, who hold a special place in my heart.

May the Holy Virgin, the Queen of Peace, speed the moment of reconciliation in all the Balkans and let the deeply desired time of a just and lasting peace in mutual respect and solidarity open up to all.

CFU 100th ANNIVERSARY BANQUET
WESTIN WILLIAM PENN HOTEL, PITTSBURGH, PA
SUNDAY, AUGUST 21, 1994

Brothers and Sisters: In our lives, we can all select moments and days which have been captured unforgettably in our memories, particularly occasions which have brought us together with our families, such as weddings, holidays and other important celebrations. Well, today, sisters and brothers, this celebration has already become for me an indelible day among life's greatest moments, as we join together to celebrate the 100th Anniversary of our Croatian Fraternal Union of America. I truly think of all of us gathered here as family and am extremely proud all 1,200 of you have made it a priority in your lives to share in this grand celebration in tribute to the centennial birthday of our Fraternal Society. The date of August 21, 1994 will remain in my memory, and I hope in yours, as a spectacular celebration of the achievements of all who have worked and believed in the Croatian Fraternal Union in the past century.

We have been blessed with the presence of His Eminence Cardinal Franjo Kuharić, Most Reverend Bishop Wuerl, President of the Parliament of the Republic of Croatia Dr. Mihanović, Prof. Dr. Katica Ivanišević, President House of Counties, many of our former CFU National officers and countless other distinguished guests from the Republic of Croatia, from the city of Pittsburgh and throughout the United States and Canada. We look with gratitude upon all of you who have come to share in this CFU Centennial Celebration with us and are truly proud to have participated in the special Mass commemorating this day and to join in this dinner which brings us together for an evening of enjoyment.

We may all proudly share in the culmination of 100 years of fraternal progress, a milestone of undeniable achievement for all of us, since in the past century our members have triumphed over great adversity and hardship in building our fraternal society and in preserving our Croatian culture and heritage on the American continent. Our early Croatian immigrants and founding fathers travelled under difficult conditions to reach America, with many passing through Ellis Island with only the few belongings they could carry from their past to sustain

Children's *tamburica* festival in Pittsburgh, a celebration to mark the centenary of the Croatian Fraternal Union

them in their new home. They struggled to overcome the tremendous barriers of language and social differences and sought to build a good life and home in this new land, yet longing to keep their Croatian heritage an integral part of their lives.

What these early immigrants carried in their hearts is alive and well in all of us today. Sisters and brothers, I am humbly proud to be an American, but I am also fiercely proud of my Croatian heritage. I know you, too, share this pride because it is what has brought us all here today and is what has built our Society to its current stature in the fraternal benefit system.

In 1894 our founding fathers realized the risks yet persevered to create an organization for the protection and benefit of our early Croatian immigrants and families. Now in 1994, it is incumbent upon us to accept the challenges of today, to safeguard the benefits of our members and to protect our Croatian heritage for generations to come as we begin this second century of our fraternal family.

The Croatian Fraternal Union of America has a bright future. To our credit, we have a diligent administration, a solid volunteer recruiter force, an established network of concerned members promoting our Croatian culture and a firm foundation which was built by our founders and cultivated by the fraternal leaders and members who have brought us to this point in time.

With gratitude and sincerity, I think each of you for helping to bring our Society to the doorstep of its 100th Anniversary. I know all of my colleagues in the national administration of the Croatian Fraternal Union join me in extending this appreciation to each of you for the unity of membership which has made this possible. Just as our pioneering immigrant fathers opened the doors of opportunity to us, so must we do the same in this second century of the Croatian Fraternal Union of America. Our one-hundred-year commitment to family and fraternalism is the focus of our celebration tonight and is the key to our success of tomorrow. In unity we began ten decades ago – and in unity we will continue for generations to follow. With respect for the principles and traditions of our forefathers, we salute the Centennial Anniversary of our fraternal family and take pride in assuming our rightful place together, as the pioneers of the second century of the Croatian Fraternal Union of America. Thank you, sisters and brothers.

Adria Croatian folklore group, Oshawa

Croatia folklore group, Mississauga

Dubrovnik Croatian folk dancing group, London, St Thomas
Zrinski-Frankopan Croatian folklore group, Richmond Hill, Ontario

Canadian-Croatian folklore festival, Montreal, 1994

Croatian woman
from Dobrota,
Boka Kotorska,
in old lace cap

Croatian women
from the
surroundings of
Subotica

Croats from Mohacs, Hungary

Croatian woman from north Burgenland, Austria

Croatian woman from Karaševo, Romania

Croatian women from Stinjak, south Burgenland, Austria

Croatian women from Kraljeva Sutjeska, the seat of Croatian rulers in Bosnia before the Turkish invasion in the 15th c., today banished from their homeland

Croatian women from Dubrava in west Slovakia

The publishers would like to thank the below mentioned for their support:

ZAGREBAČKA BANKA d.d. Zagreb
PARTNER BANKA d.d. Zagreb
"AWT INTERNATIONAL" d.o.o. Zagreb

Early-Christian basilica in Povlje on Brač, 5th c.

St *Mary Formoza* (chapel), Pula, 6th c.

St *Ambroze*, Nin, 13th c.

St *Jerome*, Split (on Marjan), 15th c.

Early-Croatian Romanesque church on Brač, 11th c.

St *Michael*, Rogovo, reconstructed in 1375